KU-072-605

mag-art

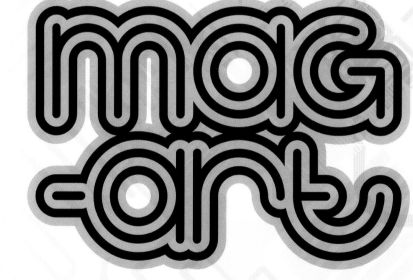

Innovation in Magazine Design

Charlotte Rivers

RotoVision

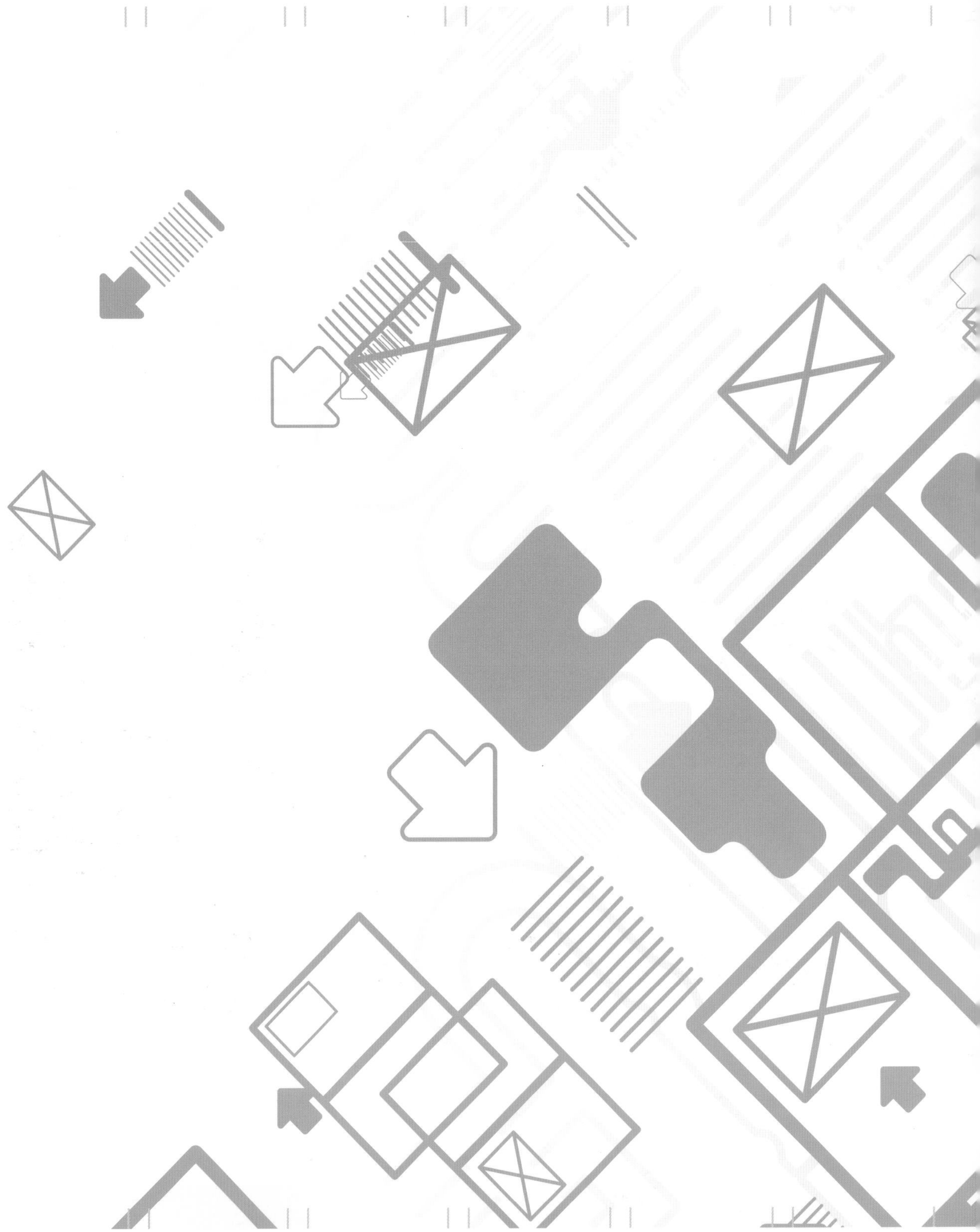

mag-art

Innovation in Magazine Design

Charlotte Rivers

BLACKBURN COLLEGE
LIBRARY
Acc.No. BB05731
Class No. HSC 741.652 RIV
Date Mar07

A RotoVision Book

Published and distributed by RotoVision SA
Route Suisse 9
CH-1295 Mies
Switzerland

RotoVision SA
Sales and Editorial Office
Sheridan House, 114 Western Road
Hove BN3 1DD, UK

Tel: +44 (0)1273 72 72 68
Fax: +44 (0)1273 72 72 69
www.rotovision.com

Copyright © RotoVision SA 2006

All rights reserved. No part of this publication may be reproduced, stored in a retrieval system, or transmitted in any form or by any means, electronic, mechanical, photocopying, recording or otherwise, without permission of the copyright holder.

While every effort has been made to contact owners of copyright material produced in this book, we have not always been successful. In the event of a copyright query, please contact the Publisher.

10 9 8 7 6 5 4 3 2 1
ISBN: 2-940361-42-8

Art Director: Tony Seddon
Design: Simon Slater, www.laki139.com
Photography: Xavier Young

Reprographics in Singapore by ProVision Pte. Ltd.
Tel: +65 6334 7720
Fax: +65 6334 7721
Printed in China by Midas Printing International Ltd.

Contents

01

"If, one day, I end up taking the plunge, I hope I will do it with strong logistical and financial backup, but most of all with the lucidity that this is not a fantasy job."

Marc Atlan, Art Director, Big: Los Angeles VIP special

Introduction

The magazine industry today is an exciting one. Not only has there never been such a variety of titles catering for so many different markets, they are also successfully pushing the boundaries of editorial design. It is not necessarily within the mainstream that this is happening—although there are exceptions—it is within the countless independent magazines from all over the world that have been launched in recent years. However they are described—microzine, fanzine, magazine, or independent magazine—these publications all have one thing in common: they have upped the magazine-design ante and are now leading the way in creative magazine design. From the creative London-based Amelia's magazine to the experimental +rosebud from Switzerland and French fashion alternative self service (one of the originals), the shelves of art bookstores are today filled with a vast array of innovative, intelligent, irreverent, and visually inspiring magazines.

A number of factors have contributed to this publishing phenomenon, including falling production costs, improved distribution, technological developments, an abundance of creative art directors and editors, and, of course, a demand for such niche titles, of which there is a great deal. These magazines present some of the most cutting-edge, innovative, and creative graphic design and art direction around today. Editorial content covers many subjects, from music to art to fashion to lifestyle to design to writing. Many have low print runs and sell in small numbers to a selective audience, and typically are only available in specialist bookstores or at selected boutiques, so echoing the "Long Tail" effect, a term first coined by Chris Anderson in a 2004 article in Wired magazine: "The theory of the 'Long Tail' is that our culture and economy is increasingly shifting away from a focus on a relatively small number of 'hits' (mainstream products and markets) at the head of the demand curve and toward a huge number of niches in the tail."

These magazines have become central to many people's lives. Stacked on the shelves of offices, studios, and homes around the world, they are where we get our cultural currency, where we look for inspiration, ideas, information, and entertainment. Importantly, they document and record cultural trends from style, design, and fashion to movements in music; to imagine a world without them seems impossible. Through their design and popularity they have established a strong market for themselves as collectible pieces of art, highly prized and treasured by many. Their content, design, and production values are so high that it's hard to throw them away. The pioneers of such design-led magazine publishing in the twentieth century are many, and each has challenged the traditional concept of magazine design in their own way. There was Nova, which ran from 1964 to 1975, and which was briefly back on our newsstands when it relaunched in 2000; i-D, which started in 1980 with 40 pages of fashion and style held together with three staples; Ray Gun, first published in California in 1992 and art directed by David Carson, who abandoned conventional magazine design, so creating one of the most innovative magazines to date; the aforementioned self service; and the influential, cult style magazine Dazed & Confused.

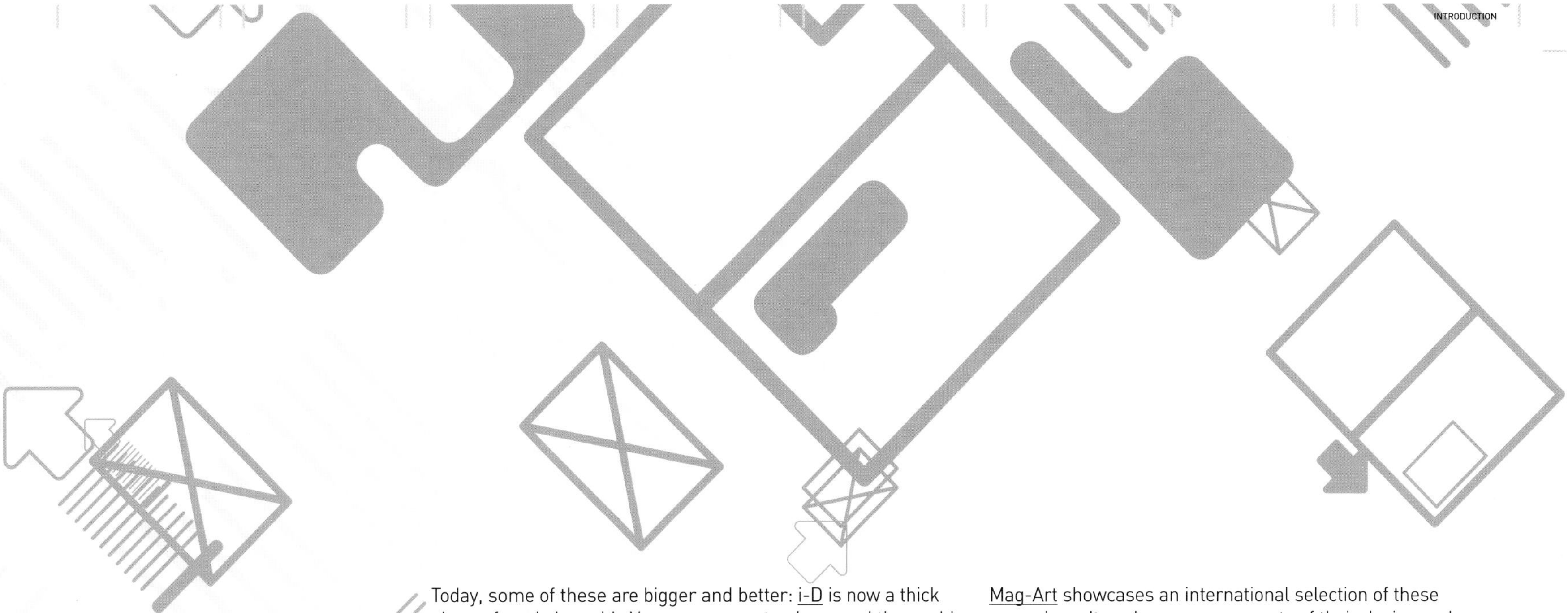

Today, some of these are bigger and better: i-D is now a thick glossy, found alongside Vogue on newsstands around the world, featuring some of the best writers and fashion photographers of the last 25 years, and continuing to have a massive influence on designers, photographers, journalists, and culture in general. Some, however, are now defunct—Nova ceased production a year after its relaunch and Ray Gun folded in 2000—while many others have come and gone, including The Face, Sleazenation, Pil, and lab.

However, plenty of titles continue to arrive, thus keeping the magazine industry on its toes. First, there are many that carry the lo-fi, do-it-yourself design esthetic of the fanzine, yet are immaculately produced publications. These may feature advertising or have some sort of low-key brand sponsorship to fund production, but many are still nonprofit and distributed free in bars, record stores, and selected fashion outlets. Examples of such are Good For Nothing and Full Moon Empty Sports Bag, both published in London, and VICE magazine, originally from Montreal, but now headquartered in New York. Then there are what many describe as microzines, the independently published magazines that survive on advertising and a higher-than-average cover price. Often with high-spec production, these are rivaling the fashion glossies, with titles like London-based Tank, which has been in production since 1998, and the internationally acclaimed Big magazine. And then there are the likes of Wallpaper* and the recently redesigned GQ Style that, despite their mainstream status, continue to challenge the design norms.

Mag-Art showcases an international selection of these magazines. It explores many aspects of their design and production, from the creative work—including artwork, typography, paper stock, format, and printing techniques—to the practical side of things, such as advertising, navigation, credits, and contents. The experimentation to be found in magazines internationally is endless, with intricately die-cut covers, unusual and experimental formats, striking imagery, and challenging typographic layouts. The sheer variety of creatively outstanding titles I came across when putting this book together shows how alive and exciting the magazine-publishing industry is today. Who said print was dead?

Charlotte Rivers

02

"The cover makes half of the magazine's impact. A bad cover is barely noticeable, diluted in the crowd of other publications at a newsstand; a good cover jumps out at you."

Marc Atlan, Art Director, Big: Los Angeles VIP special

Covers & Packaging

"I try to steer away from expected cover imagery. I have used illustration, a photo I found in a dumpster, and a painting that I found in a second-hand store."

Amelia Gregory, Publisher, Editor, and Art Director, Amelia's magazine

Introduction

Many of the magazines featured in this chapter, and indeed throughout the whole book, abandon traditional cover image, layout, and overall design in favor of a more creative, clean, and visually pleasing approach. Gone are the coverlines and predictable covers of the mainstream; instead are uncluttered, striking cover designs that are more akin to books. One of the reasons for this is, of course, that the cover follows the design and art direction of the magazine in general, but another is that, because they each have their own, unique editorial twist—and their readers know this—they are not fighting to compete with similar titles and therefore don't have to shout on the outside about what is contained inside.

From photography to illustration, the covers and therefore the "looks" of these magazines are many and varied, distinct and recognizable. In many cases, the art directors take production a step forward, using innovative printing and production techniques for the packaging of their magazines. For instance, one issue of Amelia's magazine came complete with a scratch 'n' sniff cover, and New York–based GUM magazine comes packaged in a box.

Lo-fi or high spec, what they have in common is a desire to experiment, whether this be through the use of special materials, production techniques, packaging, or photography, and that is what makes them interesting. These magazines stand out for being different and for having their own distinct and individual twist. The cover and packaging is what the potential reader sees first and a good one will draw them in and engage their senses. All the covers and packaging shown in this chapter do this with great style.

Art Direction: **Giorgio De Mitri/ Patrizia Di Gioia**
Guest Art Directors: **Nicola Peressoni/ Francesco Forti/Luca Bortolotti**
Publisher: **Giorgio De Mitri**
Country: **Italy**

CUBE

CUBE was first published in 1998, and featured the work of Thierry Ledé, Ben Drury, and Giorgio De Mitri among others. No expense was spared on design and production, with the first issue designed to be a small table as well as a magazine. That trend has continued, as Giorgio De Mitri and Patrizia Di Gioia, based at Italian design agency Sartoria, continue to produce a visually rich and inspired publication.

CUBE began life as a fanzine, eventually became a full-blown magazine, and has now morphed into a bookzine. Each issue is inspired simply by De Mitri's state of mind at the time and the relationships he has with his wide and varied network of creatives and friends. He collects images and text from them over a number of months before putting them together to create the next issue.

It is a work of passion more than anything. The target audience are people De Mitri knows, as CUBE is not for sale; he distributes the magazine only to his close friends and colleagues. CUBE is a truly unique piece of work; if you can get your hands on a copy it is well worth the effort.

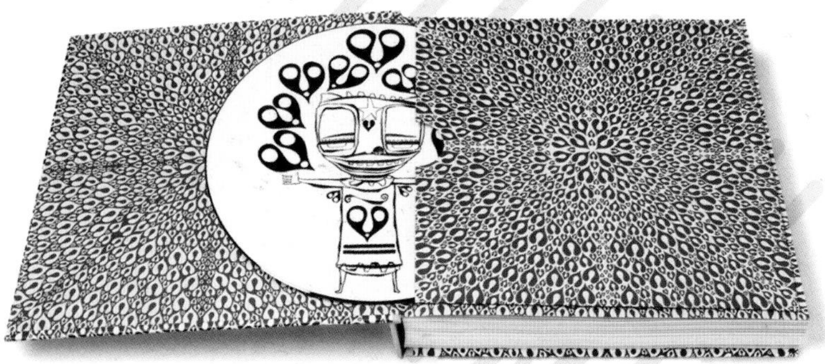

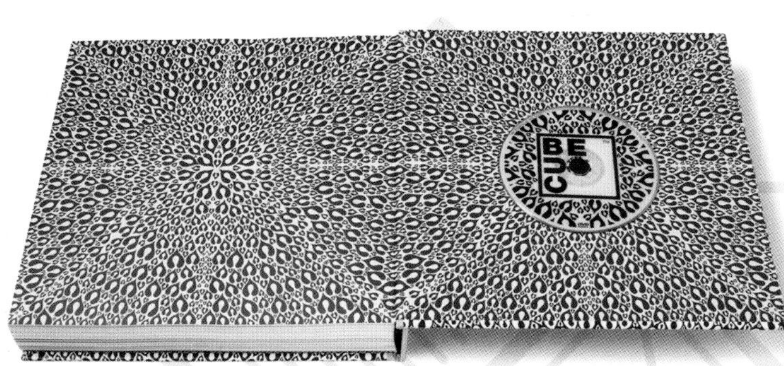

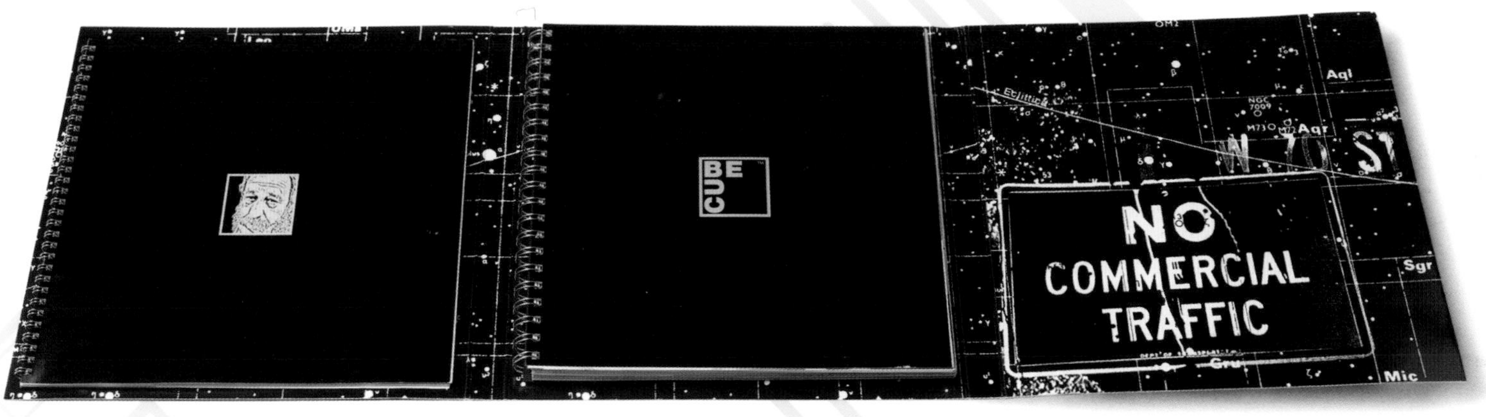
NO
COMMERCIAL
TRAFFIC

BE
CUBE
TM

Art Direction: **VICE magazine**
Design: **Inkubator.ca**
Countries: **Canada/USA**

VICE

VICE is a free, internationally distributed lifestyle magazine, founded in Canada in 1994 by Suroosh Alvi, Shane Smith, and Gavin McInnes, but currently headquartered in New York. Since its launch it has become the cult magazine of a new generation—one that shuns mainstream culture and celebrity—and it is known for its irreverent, edgy, counterculture content. The UK launch issue had spot varnish on the cover to create a "mirror," which set the magazine up for a huge media reaction and interest, but also attracted a large and dedicated readership, mainly of 18 to 34 year olds. Distributed free in bars, fashion stores, and music stores around the world, it is the counterpoint to the overdesigned, self-indulgent, graphically redundant style-magazine sector. Its esthetic is deliberately stripped down, with spare design principles and unfussy photography, and its content is humorous—for some controversial—with features like "The VICE Guide to Eating Pussy" and "The VICE Guide to Finding Yourself." Today, 11 editors around the globe create the magazine each month, and the VICE brand has expanded from print to producing records, DVDs, TV content, movies, books, online content, broadcast production and marketing, and events.

Art Direction: **Suzanne Koller/Ezra Petronio (Work in Progress)**
Publisher: **Ezra Petronio**
Country: **France**

self service

When self service magazine was founded, the aim was to create a vehicle through which writers, stylists, and photographers could express their views on fashion, the arts, and consumer culture. As founder and Art Director Ezra Petronio explains, in the 1990s, "unemployment was high and the economy was suffering. Despite this, it was an exciting time and the perfect backdrop to spark a reaction; the dance scene, driven by Daft Punk, exploded, and young European designers, such as Viktor & Rolf and Raf Simons, were keen to present their collections in the French capital."

Since then self service has provided a launch pad for many designers and it has continued to collaborate with that generation's most promising talent. Despite the fact that the magazine has now become one of the leading fashion titles, the publishers have tried hard to remain true to their original objective: to champion progressive, creative thinking and creative ideas whether they be about fashion or not. Recently, the magazine has become more booklike, with a bound format, and a hardback, textured cover.

The magazine not only features some of the world's best photography and art direction, it also includes in-depth interviews and critical writing. "We provide a transitional phase where we take raw talent and help them develop so that they can move on," explains Petronio. "If you look at any influential designer, stylist, hair, or makeup artist, at one point they started out at self service, i-D, or Dazed & Confused."

REALITY TV

ALEXIA LAROCHE-JOUBERT

DIRECTOR OF PROGRAMMING, ENDEMOL FRANCE

ON STAR ACADEMY, LOFT STORY AND THE REALITY OF REALITY TV. ON REALITY TV'S ORIGINS IN THE WORLD OF FINE ARTS.

PARIS, JANUARY 11TH, [illegible]

Conversation with Eric [illegible]. Photography by Katja Rahlwes

Taking over as head designer of a fashion house is often not all it's cracked up to be. In recent years, we have seen fresh and sometimes unready talent parachuted in and almost as quickly ejected out of one luxury brand after another. Pressured to either re-interpret the past or create something radically different, the dilemma remains how to remain faithful to a brand and yet continue to bring it into new territories. Yves Saint Laurent has always symbolized a certain untouchable elegance and sophistication almost lost under Tom Ford, but which Stefano Pilati, design director since April, 2004, has gotten just right. Having assisted Ford after passing through the schools of Giorgio Armani and Miuccia Prada, Stefano has remained humble after taking over as design director of YSL, surely and discreetly luring back the fans of Monsieur and gaining the trust of the market. As with the namesake of the house, his designs show an impeccable sleekness, a respect for women and a true understanding of elegance. He speaks with Ezra Petronio and Suzanne Koller about youth; the substance of experience; feminine freedom; avoiding vulgarity; gender roles; pacing oneself; the importance of fashion's voice on social change; heritage versus the future; celebrating a Parisian attitude; and nostalgia for what has not yet come to pass.

Art Direction: **Kevin Grady/Colin Metcalf**
Publishers: **Kevin Grady/Colin Metcalf**
Country: **USA**

GUM

GUM Publishers and Art Directors Kevin Grady and Colin Metcalf both have backgrounds in art and journalism, but neither had been involved in the overall production of a magazine, so, in 2002, they decided to create one that would offer something new and different to readers. "Modern media has consolidated steadily under the grip of fewer and larger corporate entities, so the content and expression we have access to is increasingly limited, and tends to revolve narrowly around celebrity, fashion, and entertainment," they explain. "We wanted to break the paradigm and hopefully provide something unique that communicates both individuality and respect to an underserved and overlooked audience—a culturally aware and curious set, aged 18–45, students and professionals in the creative realms of design, broadcast, film, advertising, and so on."

What Grady and Metcalf have done with GUM is to create a complete package. Each issue comes wrapped in its own specially designed package, making them highly collectible items. The idea is to make the magazine feel like a gift. Issue 1 came with bubble gum and stickers, and Issue 2 with bubble gum and a ViewMaster reel.

Each issue is clearly thought out before design and production begins, from the color palettes to the pacing, typography, and editorial voice. This adds a real complexity to the mixture of vector art and photographs, clean typography, and textured graphics within GUM. Grady and Metcalf have worked with many photographers and illustrators on these issues—including Jeanne Hilary, Guido Vitti, Steven Barston, Greg Ruhl, Steve Illing, and Jeff Ramras—to produce some great design and editorial content.

GUM, features modified DIN Schriften for the body text and GUM for the headline font, created specifically for this purpose. GUM 2 features Apex Sans as body text and Transectional for the headline, again designed by Grady and Metcalf specifically for the job. So what's the best thing about designing and publishing a magazine? "Having control over the presentation and content of this magazine is great," they say.

...AND WITH JON SPENCER, WHOSE BAND BLUES EXPLOSION IS FAMOUS FOR A MUSICAL FERVOR AND SWEAT-DRENCHED PERFORMANCES THAT BORDER ON, WELL... POSSESSED
TONIGHT THOUGH, JON IS SEDATE. INSTEAD OF TAKING A MUCH-NEEDED DAY OFF HE'S TALKING TO US.
I FIRST SAW THE PLASTIC MAN BOOK THAT CHIP DID* IN A COMIC BOOK SHOP ACROSS FROM OUR HOTEL IN L.A. WHEN WE WERE MASTERING "PLASTIC FANG", AND I BOUGHT IT LATER IN SEATTLE.
WHEN I CAME BACK TO N.Y. I WAS OUT WITH A FRIEND WHO HAD A CONNECTION WITH CHIP SO I GOT HIS EMAIL ADDRESS AND THEN...
*JACK COLE: PLASTIC MAN: FORMS STRETCHED TO THEIR LIMITS" BY ART SPIEGELMAN & CHIP KIDD
POP CARD
PHIL FROST
FUN FACT:
THE SOLITAIRE IS THE STRONGEST OF DIAMONDS; A SINGLE GEM ABLE TO WITHSTAND THE MOST PRESSURE AND REFLECT THE MOST LIGHT.
STATS:
BORN: February 7, 1973
HOMETOWN: ?
CURRENT HOME: Upstate New York
PET SOUNDS: I have a cat, Thor, who purrs in interesting patterns, and the medallion on his collar clanks when he eats from a bowl or plate
EATS: Sushi, greens, mangos with chili powder
SLEEPS: A full night's rest
DRINKS: Juiced vegetable elixirs, water
RIGHTY/LEFTY: ?
WINDOW/AISLE: All-Inner-Souls-Live-Eternally
GUX
POP STAR
ANIMAL LOVER
GUM
KOSTAS SEREMETIS

Art Direction: **Ralf Herms**
Publisher: **Ralf Herms**
Countries: **Germany/Austria**

+rosebud

+rosebud was first published by Ralf Herms in Austria in 1998 as a graduation project. It has grown into a stunningly designed magazine/book. For each issue Herms selects a theme and then invites people from many different creative professions—including designers, photographers, illustrators, sociologists, poets, sculptors, actors, and design students—to approach the specific topic in their own way. For Issue 4, "Action," Herms sent out a book to every potential contributor. In each he buried a used camera film by cutting through the center of the book. The instructions were to get the film developed and find the brief within the resulting photographs. The images on each of the film rolls were identical. Herms and his team shot them in the same order from a slideshow on a computer screen.

Once all the work came in, Herms began a long editing process to select which contributions to include, and put them together to form a complete issue. The production for this issue is particularly interesting. The magazine is very much in book format. It has a clothbound, hardboard outer cover inside which the pages of the magazine, also clothbound, are placed. The bottom of the spine features a thumb punch of about 1in (25mm) square which creates an endearing flick book with a skipping character by artist Kojo Griffin. When removed, this leaves a cut-out section across the gutter, as shown on page 23. A page of stickers is also included.

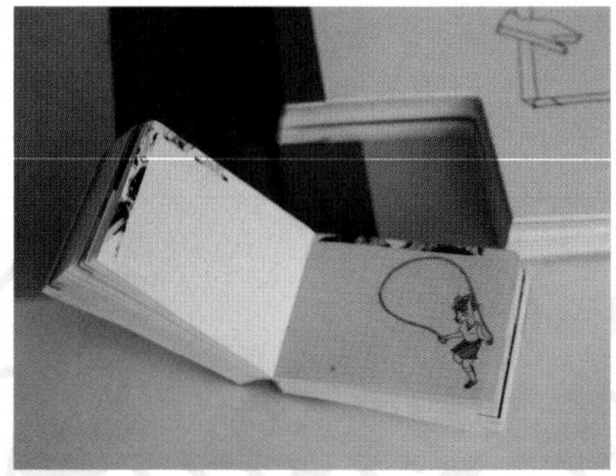

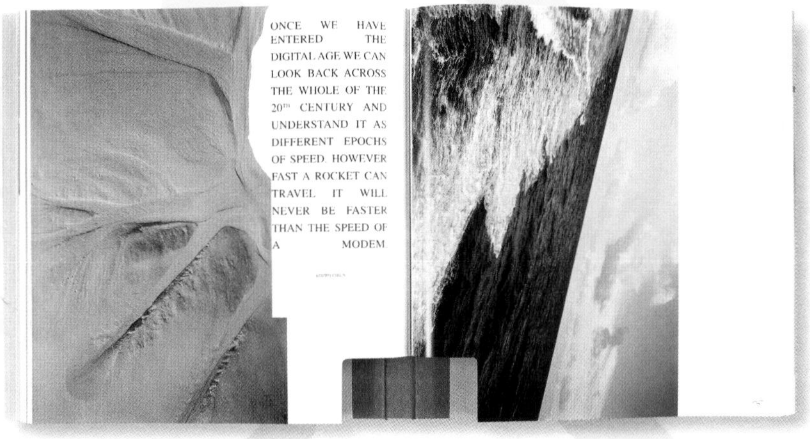
ONCE WE HAVE ENTERED THE DIGITAL AGE WE CAN LOOK BACK ACROSS THE WHOLE OF THE 20TH CENTURY AND UNDERSTAND IT AS DIFFERENT EPOCHS OF SPEED. HOWEVER FAST A ROCKET CAN TRAVEL IT WILL NEVER BE FASTER THAN THE SPEED OF A MODEM.

204=CC
174=AE

Art Direction: **Amelia Gregory**
Publisher: **Amelia Gregory**
Country: **UK**

Amelia's magazine

The first issue of Amelia's magazine was published in Spring/Summer 2004. It featured musician Pete Doherty's prison diaries and an exclusive Doherty track produced as a flexi-disk and packaged with the magazine. It has since grown into one of the most interesting and experimental magazines around. Shown on these pages are Issues 2 and 4 from Autumn/Winter 2004 and 2005, respectively.

Issue 2 was designed by Scot Bendall and Asger Bruun. It came complete with a die-cut cover (designed by Rob Ryan) and a Tatty Devine pendant which was nestled in the magazine by die cutting a hole into the first 18 pages. Issue 4 was fully interactive, featuring a scratch-and-sniff cover (which takes you right back to childhood) and smelly pens customized with the Amelia's magazine logo. These are intended for use in coloring in the illustrated pictures provided inside the magazine.

Despite these touches, Amelia's magazine has a distinctly lo-fi design esthetic. It uses matte finish stock throughout, spray-painted stencil typefaces, countless illustrations, and handwritten text. Publisher Amelia Gregory does not start with a particular idea for each issue; the design and production evolves naturally. "There was no specific idea behind each different issue of the magazine and the design and layouts happen organically. I don't think too hard about them, they just kind of happen," she explains.

Issue 3—shown on page 26—demonstrates how advertising can be made to be not only engaging, but also interactive. Designed by Hassan Tagiuri, this issue came with a flock-effect cover—the image of the dog was found by Gregory in a thrift store—and a page of stickers, each one created by different illustrators.

However, what is particularly interesting is the advertisement placed in the magazine by Levi's for its Patty Anne jeans. The ad is over a double-page spread that has been stitched together at the edge so the reader has to pull the pages apart to see what is inside. It reflects the Levi's campaign that ran at that time and which featured images of the jeans stitched into the bodies of the models. It is a clever and engaging feature of the magazine, but retains the lo-fi feel of each issue by appearing handstitched.

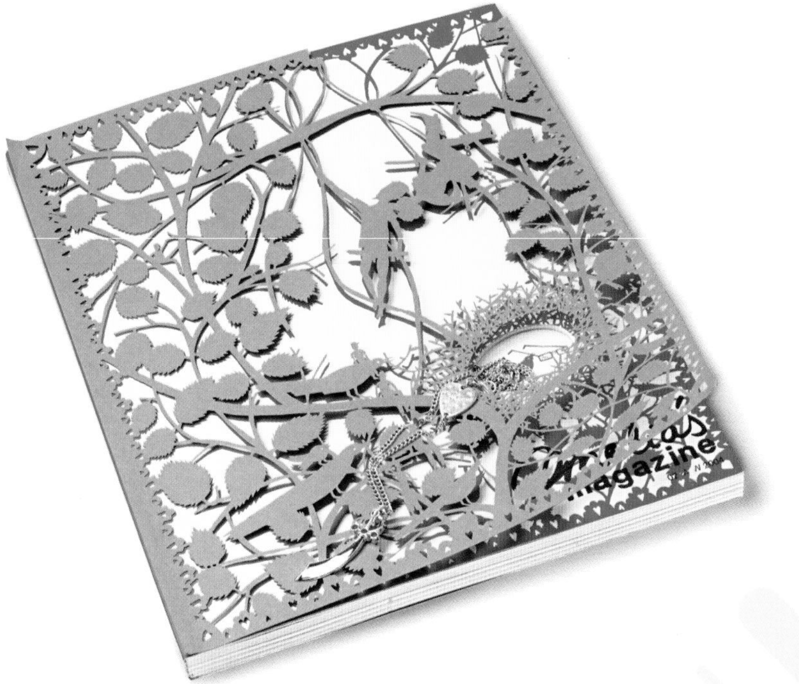

RITON

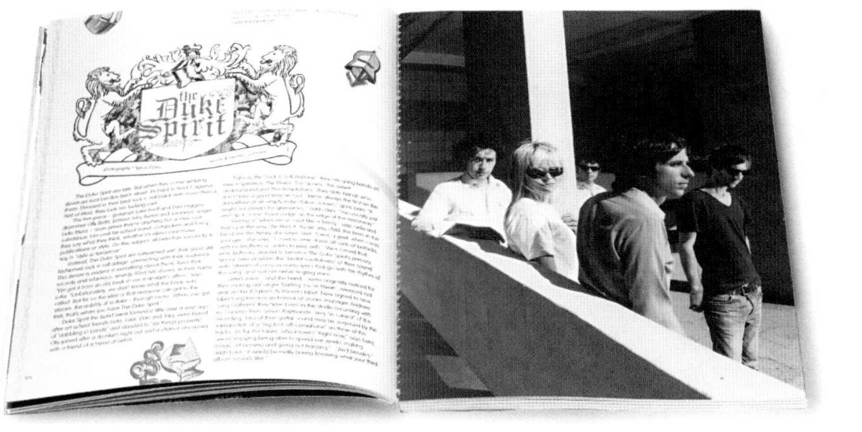
the Duke Spirit

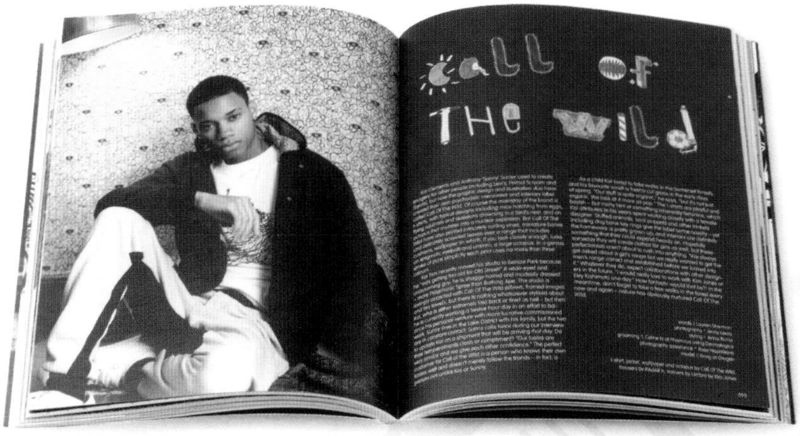
Call of The Wild

£9.99
Amelia's
magazine
03 S/S 2005

Hello dear reader

ghost
YOU WILL NEED
BODY
ARMS
BALL & CHAIN
RATTLE
TO MAKE UP THE GHOST

CAN'T PULL 'EM APART
PATTY ANNE SLIM FIT JEAN

Art Direction: **Rebecca Smith**
Publisher: **Independent**
Country: **UK**

Lula

In the words of Lula Editor Leith Clark, "This is a magazine about things we love." It is a fashion and lifestyle magazine with a difference, in that its intention is to not take itself too seriously. Inspired by memories from childhood—dressing up and story-books—it takes a playful and ethereal approach to art, fashion, and movies.

Clark and Art Director Rebecca Smith had been approached to give an existing magazine a makeover, but halfway through the job decided to go solo and start from scratch to create an entirely new publication. Shown here is their first issue, which features collaborations with, among others, Blossom Berkofsky, Nicky Peacock, Poppy de Villeneuve, Dan Jackson, and Drew Jarrett. It's a great addition to the fashion-magazine market: simple, approachable, cute, and girlie, all at the same time.

Art Direction: **Discover Upnorth**
Publisher: **Discover Upnorth**
Country: **USA**

oneonenine

oneonenine is a graphic design and art-magazine collaboration organized by New York-based designers Justin Kay and Steve Green, otherwise known as Discover Upnorth. Essentially the magazine—the first issue of which is shown here—started by featuring the work of friends of Kay and Green, but they want to expand this idea to incorporate the work of other designers and artists from around the world. Contributors to this issue include Grotesk, Knuckle Duster, Prate, We Work For Them, and Design By Build.

The format is fanzine size of—7 x 8½in (178 x 216mm)—and a limited run of 300 copies were produced. It is nonprofit and features no advertising, but has a cover price to accommodate print and production costs. The first issue came packaged in a sealed plastic bag with graphically illustrated magnets included. Printing has been kept minimal, using only black and green inks on white. Akzidenz Grotesk typeface has been used throughout to keep the text clean and simple, complementing the often busy and bold artwork featured.

119: ISSUE 1
EDITION:
Salad Days
FIRESIDE BOWL
brian mackin
tragicbalance.com

119: ISSUE 1
EDITION:
Lick a Shot
25¢
TO PLAY!
WISH YOU WEREN'T HERE
LOVE PK
PK

119: ISSUE 1
EDITION:
GREEN CARD DENIED.
grotesk
grotesk.to

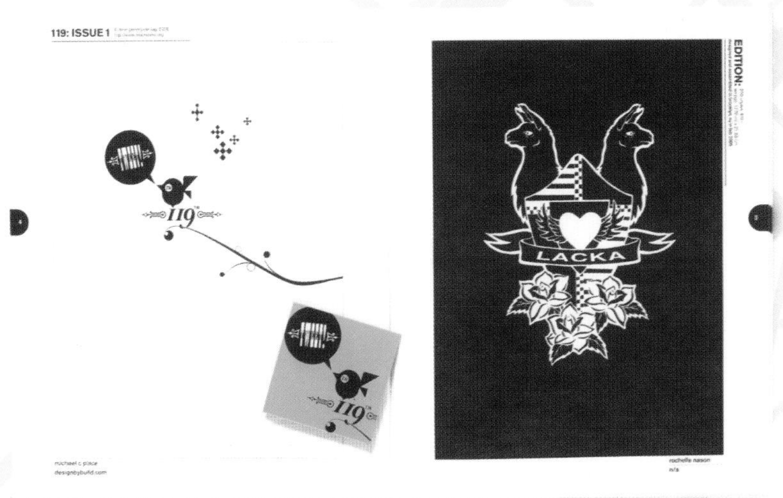
119: ISSUE 1
EDITION:
119
LACKA

Art Direction: **Patrick Duffy**
Publishers: **Patrick Duffy/Steve Cotton/ Ian Allison**
Photography: **Steve Cotton**
Illustration: **Chris Graham**
Country: **UK**

Full Moon Empty Sports Bag

Full Moon Empty Sports Bag was started in London in 2003 by Patrick Duffy, Steve Cotton, and Ian Allison. It concentrates on areas they feel are left vacant by the mainstream magazine press, principally short fiction and poetry. It has become a popular read, featuring the work of many known and unknown writers and poets, including musician Pete Doherty of UK bands The Libertines and Babyshambles.

The publishers receive much unsolicited material for the magazine. "It is always charming to receive poetry through the post," explains Duffy. "Poetry occupies this weird anachronistic and hallowed place in our culture and it is always nice to be on the receiving end of this."

The art direction of each issue is considered in its own right, and there are no rules, although what is consistent is that each issue has a lo-fi feel. Photography and imagery are experimental: as shown here. The cover of Issue 12: Medicine features a model wrapped in bandages. Each time the image is shown in the magazine, more bandages are removed to reveal some disturbing images beneath.

The magazine's original format was A5 (5¾ x 8¼ in/148 x 210mm) saddle stitched, but that changed with Issue 13 and the introduction of a unique binding technique. Essentially Issue 13 is two 32-page sections saddle-stitched together to form a double-length cover as shown below. This issue has to be read by turning the pages of the right- and left-hand sections simultaneously, so each time you are revealing four new pages rather than the usual two. "We took on this binding technique for a number of reasons. First, we wanted to expand and give our readers more content, but had no budget to go to a perfect bind, which increases the cost of printing considerably," explains Duffy. "Also, we didn't want to follow the same route as everyone else, so looked for other ways to expand while remaining unique. It was a good design challenge to work on four-page spreads."

Full Moon Empty Sports Bag
#12
"If there had been no doctors there would never have been any sick people, no dead skeletons, sick people to be butchered and flayed, for it was with doctors and not with sick people that society began."
ANTONIN ARTAUD

Matt Cartmell
A Job Done Properly
14 FEBRUARY
27 MARCH
4 APRIL
18 APRIL

Art Direction: **Dave Eggers/Eli Horowitz**
Publisher: **McSweeney's**
Country: **USA**

McSweeney's

McSweeney's is a quarterly magazine that features short stories, and always comes in interesting formats with unusual and unique designs. It was started by Dave Eggers, who recognized the need for a place to put all the good short stories and other writing he came across. "There seemed to be a lot of good work without a home," explains McSweeney's Managing Director Eli Horowitz, "and Dave wanted to create a context for all these varied stories to be shown in."

Shown here are two great examples of this "journal's" design. For Issue 16 they wanted to create something that looked like a book, but unfolded unexpectedly, and for Issue 17 they wanted to replicate a bundle of junk mail, both ideas that have been successfully executed to a very high and considered finish. Garamond 3 typeface is used "as much as possible" throughout the magazine for its readability and flexibility.

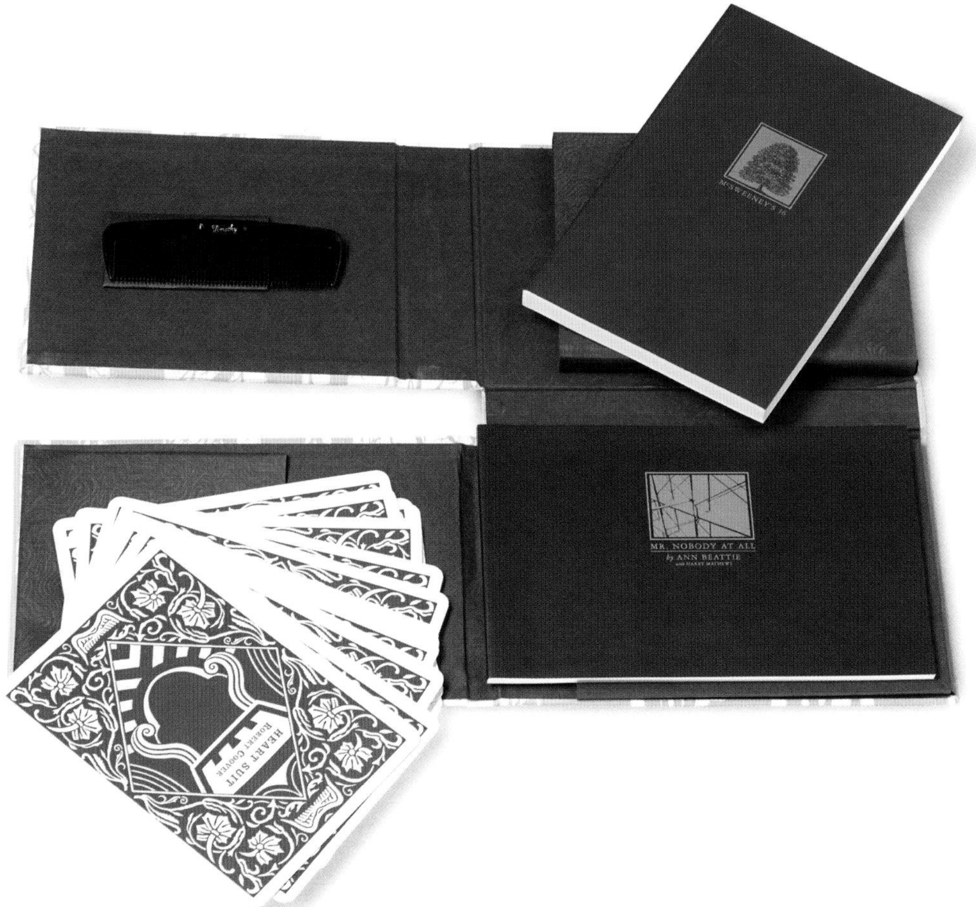

ENVELOPE
SPORTSWEAR CLEARANCE DAYS
PANTALAINE
McSWEENEY'S 17
MADE TO LOOK LIKE IT CAME IN YOUR MAILBOX
unisex snap trainer
$29
women's all-cotton jogger

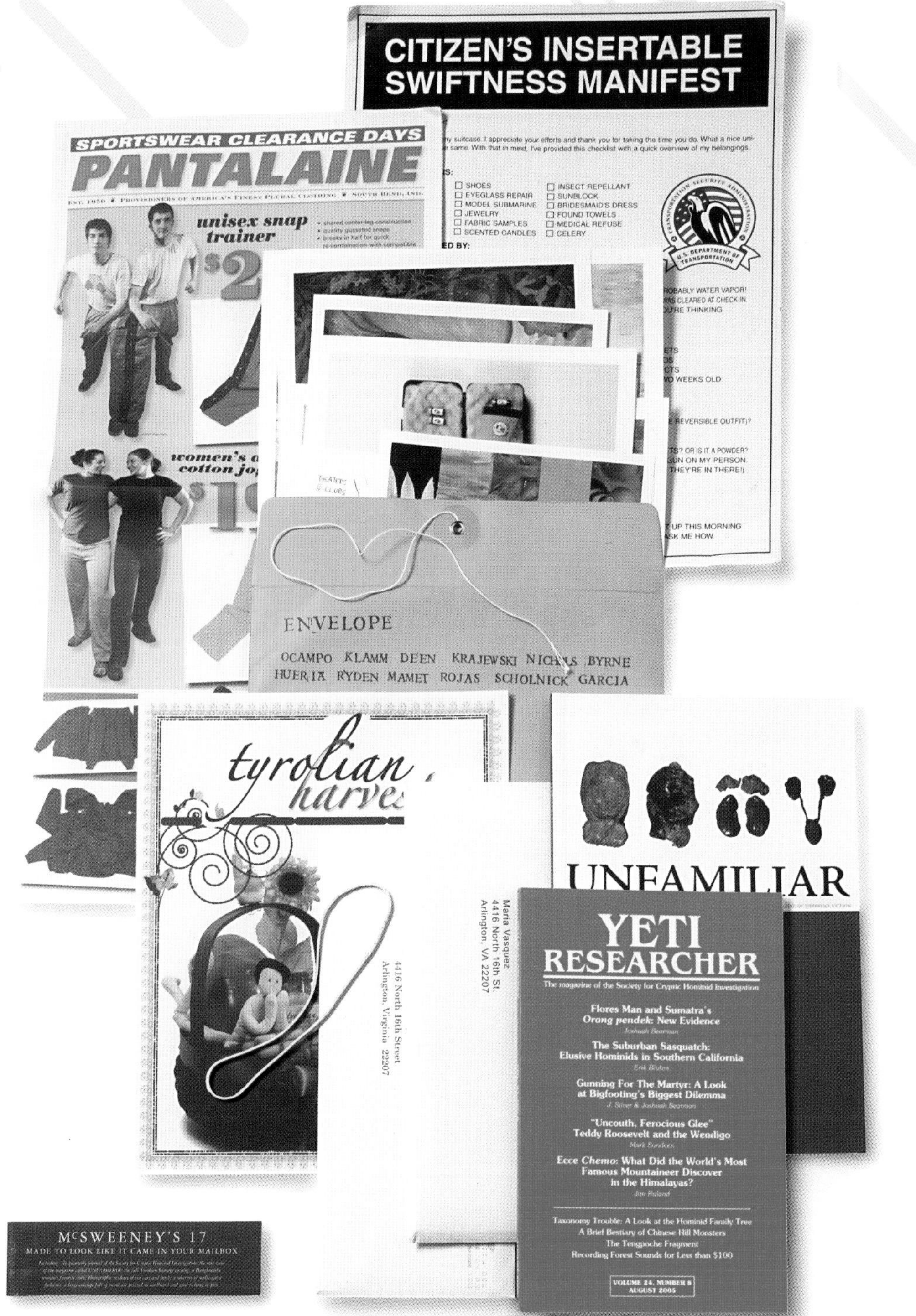
CITIZEN'S INSERTABLE SWIFTNESS MANIFEST
SHOES
EYEGLASS REPAIR
MODEL SUBMARINE
JEWELRY
FABRIC SAMPLES
SCENTED CANDLES
INSECT REPELLANT
SUNBLOCK
BRIDESMAID'S DRESS
FOUND TOWELS
MEDICAL REFUSE
CELERY
U.S. DEPARTMENT OF TRANSPORTATION
SPORTSWEAR CLEARANCE DAYS
PANTALAINE
unisex snap trainer
women's all-cotton jogger
ENVELOPE
OCAMPO KLAMM DEEN KRAJEWSKI NICHOLS BYRNE
HUERTA RYDEN MAMET ROJAS SCHOLNICK GARCIA
tyrolian harvest
4416 North 16th Street
Arlington, Virginia 22207
Maria Vasquez
4416 North 16th St.
Arlington, VA 22207
UNFAMILIAR
YETI RESEARCHER
The magazine of the Society for Cryptic Hominid Investigation
Flores Man and Sumatra's Orang pendek: New Evidence
The Suburban Sasquatch: Elusive Hominids in Southern California
Gunning For The Martyr: A Look at Bigfooting's Biggest Dilemma
"Uncouth, Ferocious Glee" Teddy Roosevelt and the Wendigo
Ecce Chemo: What Did the World's Most Famous Mountaineer Discover in the Himalayas?
Taxonomy Trouble: A Look at the Hominid Family Tree
A Brief Bestiary of Chinese Hill Monsters
The Tengpoche Fragment
Recording Forest Sounds for Less than $100
VOLUME 24, NUMBER 8
AUGUST 2005
McSWEENEY'S 17
MADE TO LOOK LIKE IT CAME IN YOUR MAILBOX

Art Direction: **LAKI 139**
Design: **LAKI 139**
Country: **UK**

AURA

AURA's aim is to bring together expressive art from our everyday environment. The magazine is a celebration of graphic communication, which has mutated and expanded from traditional graffiti art.

AURA started life as an 8-page portfolio booklet for LAKI 139. Enjoying the freedom of using paper stock of different colors and textures, mixed with conventional printing processes (LaserWriter, stencil, spray paint, and photocopier), LAKI 139 decided to publish a fanzine.

For Issue 1, LAKI 139 brought together 12 artists (old friends and new) with similar souls, but all with a unique personality in their work. Contributors ranged from graffiti artists to illustrators. "I wanted to get the feel of a sketch book instead of the work being presented polished, with a load of white space. Sketchbooks have more energy. I asked each artist to send a scan of their books to be the opening page of their work." Paper stock was carefully chosen to complement each artist's work.

Issue 1 was produced in a limited-edition of 139 copies. The 80 pages were individually French-folded, hand crafted, and Japanese bound with wax-coated cotton. Each cover is unique (see poster right), making this a highly collectible and rare first edition. For strength and durability, the covers were coated in Yacht varnish. "When I was making mock-ups I tried out the varnish on a cover. After a couple of months the cover started to change color and age. It reminded me of the old Russian avant-garde books."

LAKI 139
The desire of AURA is to bring together expressive art that 'surrounds us' in our everyday environment.
This book is a celebration of graphic communication, which has mutated and expanded from the association of traditional graffiti art. AURA has brought together twelve artists (old friends and new), with similar souls, but with unique personality in their work.
AURA is continually searching for Artist's contributions and photographs to be showcased in future issues.
For more information mail to: aura@laki139.com
This numbered limited edition book of 139, has been individually folded, hand-crafted, varnished and stitched. Each cover is unique (see below), making this a highly collectible and rare first edition.
AURA
AURA
ISSUE 1
AURA

AURA
AURA
ISSUE 1

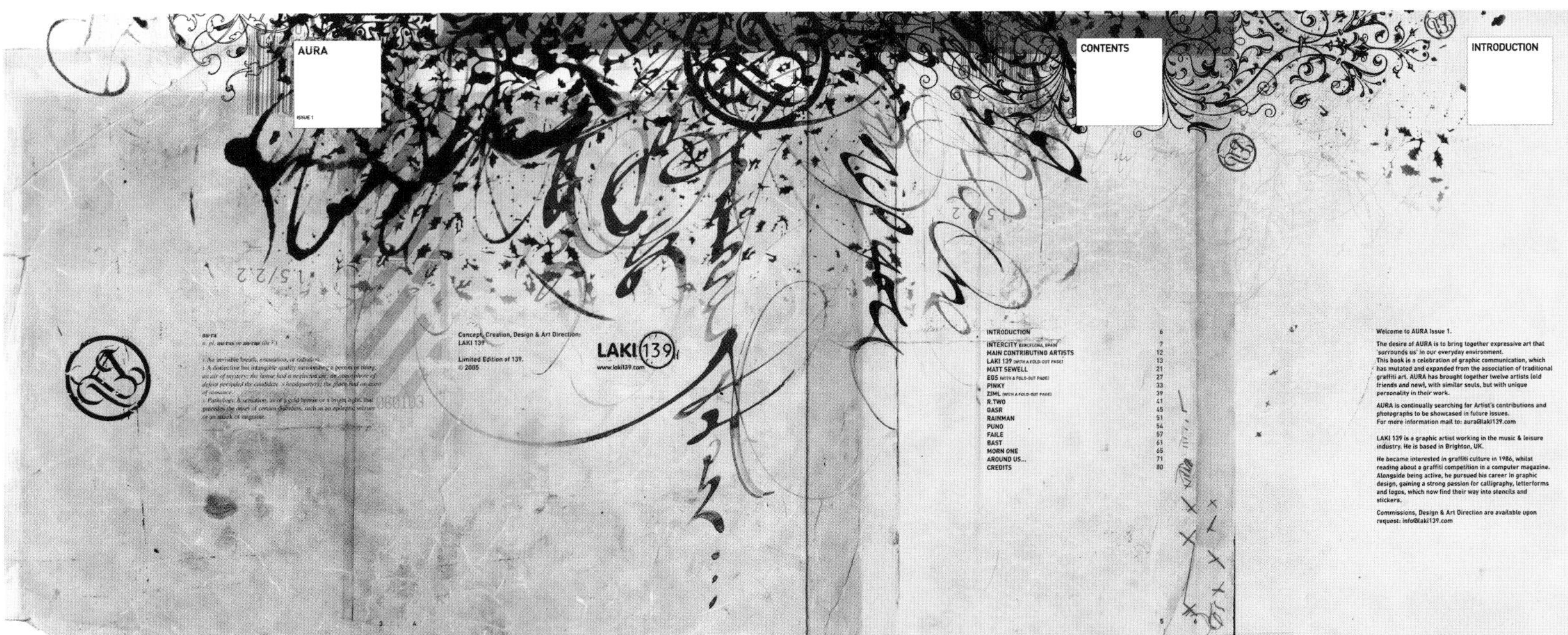
AURA
ISSUE 1
CONTENTS
INTRODUCTION
Concept, Creation, Design & Art Direction:
LAKI 139
Limited Edition of 139.
© 2005
LAKI 139
www.laki139.com
INTRODUCTION 6
INTERCITY BARCELONA, SPAIN 7
MAIN CONTRIBUTING ARTISTS 12
LAKI 139 (WITH A FOLD-OUT PAGE) 13
MATT SEWELL 21
EOS (WITH A FOLD-OUT PAGE) 27
PINKY 33
ZIML (WITH A FOLD-OUT PAGE) 39
R.TWO 41
BASR 45
RAINMAN 51
PUNO 54
FAILE 57
BAST 61
MORN ONE 65
AROUND US... 71
CREDITS 80
Welcome to AURA Issue 1.
The desire of AURA is to bring together expressive art that 'surrounds us' in our everyday environment.
This book is a celebration of graphic communication, which has mutated and expanded from the association of traditional graffiti art. AURA has brought together twelve artists (old friends and new), with similar souls, but with unique personality in their work.
AURA is continually searching for Artist's contributions and photographs to be showcased in future issues.
For more information mail to: aura@laki139.com
LAKI 139 is a graphic artist working in the music & leisure industry. He is based in Brighton, UK.
He became interested in graffiti culture in 1986, whilst reading about a graffiti competition in a computer magazine. Alongside being active, he pursued his career in graphic design, gaining a strong passion for calligraphy, letterforms and logos, which now find their way into stencils and stickers.
Commissions, Design & Art Direction are available upon request: info@laki139.com

BLACKBURN COLLEGE LIBRARY

ARTIST:
LAKI 139
MATT SEWELL
EGS
PINKY
ZIML
R.TWO
GASR
RAINMAN
PUNO
FAILE
BAST
MORN
ORIGIN:
UK
UK
FINLAND
UK
UK
UK
UK
UK
UK
USA
USA
UK
MAIN CONTRIBUTING ARTISTS
LAKI 139
www.laki139.com
MATT SEWELL
www.mattsewell.co.uk
EGS
CDC, MSN, TPG
PINKY
DRA
ZIML
DRA, TCF
R.TWO
WSR, STD
GASR
www.thegasface.co.uk
RAINMAN
PUNO
STD, RTH, RNB
FAILE
www.faile.net
BAST
info: faile@faile.net
MORN
TPG
12

RALPH, POE, EGS - 2004
EGS, ENS - FIRENZE, ITALY, 2004
PIETRO, EGS, RALPH - 2004
EGS - FIRENZE, ITALY, 2004
EGS, REIM - COPENHAGEN, DENMARK, 2004
EGS, SQAR - HELSINKI, FINLAND

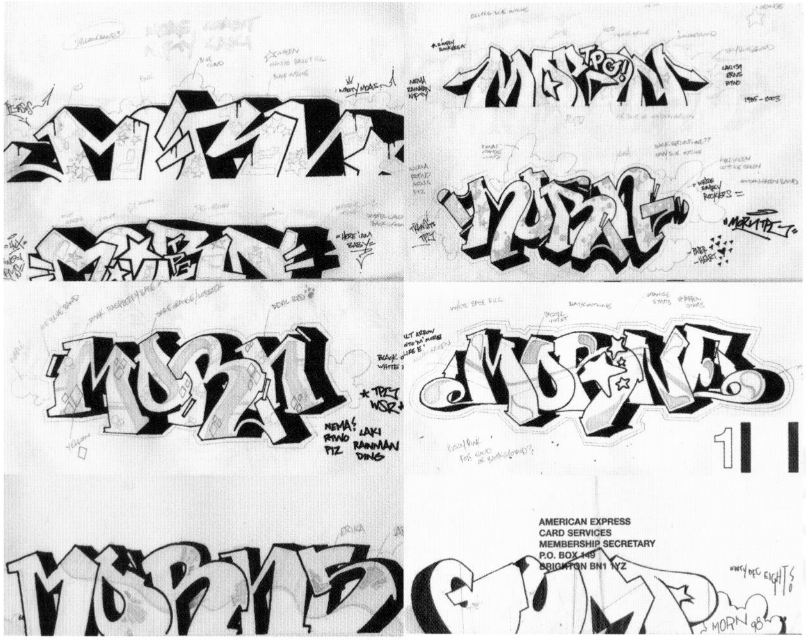
AMERICAN EXPRESS
CARD SERVICES
MEMBERSHIP SECRETARY

COLOGNE, GERMANY
COLOGNE, GERMANY
72
73

Art Direction: **Various**
Creative Direction: **Martin Lötscher**
Publisher: **Martin Lötscher/Iris Ruprecht**
Country: **Switzerland**

soDA

Swiss magazine soDA was founded in 1996. It features the work of renowned authors from the worlds of design, art, science, architecture, photography, fashion, philosophy, literature, and poetry. Published quarterly, soDA publisher Iris Ruprecht says it "offers intelligent experiences in art for opinion makers and trendsetters who are interested in the arts."

Shown here is Issue 21: Aktion. In addition to the main section in traditional format comes the thematic part in unbound sheets inside the plastic "folder" that holds it all together. Continuity in appearance is achieved by the fundamental unity of content and visualization and not by the classic magazine format with established columns and sections. As a result, soDA succeeds in having the character of a book, so something to be kept and collected.

"With soDA we want to bring artists and art lovers together and open up possibilities to break out of conventional thinking and explore new avenues," explains Ruprecht. "What we offer is an opening and a stage, freedom and challenge, task and goal, and we produce a high-quality magazine that is a collectible must-have for every bookshelf. We are nonconformist and independent, capricious and unorthodox, profound and individual, playful and serious, irritating, clarifying, and experimental."

(See page 132 for Issue 27 of soDA.)

Art Direction: **Luca Ionescu/ Michelle Hendriks**
Publisher: **Keep Left Studio**
Country: **Australia**

Refill

Refill was launched in 2003. Based in Australia, its founders felt that there was no magazine around at the time that featured the artists that they wanted to know about. It was intended to showcase the work of a range of artists and designers from different fields, from architects to movie directors to graffiti artists. Shown here are Issue 4 (below and top four spreads opposite) and Issue 5 (bottom two spreads opposite).

The design of Refill is experimental, with its packaging and format changing every issue. The design is based on the cover idea that the featured artist has. "The brief is kind of up to ourselves, so once we've invited the artists whose work we admire and want to feature, we then work with them on artwork for the cover and brainstorm ideas on how we should package the magazine," explains Art Director Michelle Hendriks. "With Issue 4 we worked with Michael Place from Build, and were inspired by industrial-packaging materials and the way other items, such as record sleeves or cereal boxes, may be packaged."

Helvetica Neue is mostly used throughout for its "clean" esthetic and the fact that it does not take away from the featured artists' work. "It's a nice simple way to complement the work without being intrusive," explains Hendriks. "We also like using Helvetica because the main focus of the articles is to communicate information about the artist, so it should be as easy to read and understand as possible."

Refill ZeroFour
Contents

118

TIMOTHY
SACCENTI
P054

EPCOT

Amelia Gregory, Publisher, Editor, and Art Director, Amelia's magazine

What is the key to art directing a magazine?
I just put together elements that I like. I guess that because I am not a trained graphic designer it is all quite instinctive. I am sure that I break a lot of rules, but I like the end result and it seems that other people do too.

Which other magazine would you most like to have the chance to art direct?
I don't want to work on anything else. The point of Amelia's magazine is that it is entirely mine. If I were to work on something else, I am sure there would be other parameters that I would have to consider and while it might be interesting, I don't think it could be as much fun as what I do when I can totally indulge my own tastes.

What is the story behind Amelia's magazine?
I can't even remember why I wanted to make my own magazine, but I went on about it to lots of people over a few years and eventually I thought I had better do it, or people would think I had cried wolf. It was initially something that I wanted to do with a friend, but she backed out, and when it became clear that I would be doing it on my own I decided that I would give it a very personal name to reflect that.

What inspires the creative idea behind each issue?
Usually the ideas come to me out of nowhere, but I am most inspired by the stuff that I collect from secondhand shops, and things that I remember enjoying from my childhood. I am inspired by random things, like books or records that I find in charity shops.

What makes Amelia's magazine different?
I would say the fact that it is produced just by me makes a big difference. I think my readers know that everything in the magazine comes from my heart. I feel passionate about the contents and I think that comes through. It's creative, personal, different, vibrant, and inspiring.

How do you begin work on each issue?
Usually I start on the advertising first, then if there is some complicated production method to sort out I will deal with that, for example, the laser-cut cover. At the same time I will be seeing potential contributors and commissioning. From then on everything happens at once and I have to juggle it all. The actual designing of the magazine happens in the last month, although I will usually be having ideas about how I would like to design it over the whole six-month period and just storing them at the back of my brain.

How do you choose a team to create each issue?
In each issue I try to work with different contributors to keep the magazine fresh. I get approached by lots of people, and I choose to work with the ones whose work I like the best.

What is important about that team?
That I like their work and think it merits space in the magazine.

How important do you think the cover image on a magazine is?
I have tried to steer away from expected cover imagery. I have used illustration, a photo that I found in a photo album in a dumpster, and a painting that I found in a secondhand shop. And I like to do something that other magazines would never do because it would be too expensive, for example, the laser-cut, detachable cover, or the flock cover, or the scratch-and-sniff cover that was printed in fluorescent inks. Hopefully the people who pick up my magazine are seduced by the unexpected cover imagery.

There are more and more really creative, well designed magazines being published for niche markets. Do you see this as the future of magazine publishing? Yes. I think if you want gossip or something immediate then it is easy to get that directly from the Internet, so there is less need for print. I made a very conscious decision to produce something of high value and tactile appeal so that people would want to feel it and own it and treasure it and be inspired by it. Amelia's magazine will never have a huge audience, but hopefully it has a faithful one.

What is your favorite magazine; what do you always buy and collect?
I don't buy any other magazines anymore. When I was younger I revered The Face, but then I worked there and it lost its appeal.

Marc Atlan, Art Director, Big: Los Angeles VIP special

Which are your three favorite magazine covers of all time?
The three magazines with my favorite covers of all time are Parkett, Six, and Lui.

Number one: It's a tie between two issues of Parkett, the contemporary art magazine: Parkett Issue 17 (1988, Peter Fischli and David Weiss) portrays a cat standing in an anthropomorphic position; and Parkett Issue 49 (1997, Douglas Gordon, Laurie Anderson, and Jeff Wall) is a mirror image of the regular layout of the cover. Both covers denote simple, ironic, humorous, and ultimately brilliant concepts.

Number two: Six, the groundbreaking fashion, photography, and culture magazine, published by famed Japanese designer Rei Kawakubo for Comme des Garçons. The 1988 to 1991, short-lived cult magazine Six has always displayed the strangest yet most attractive covers. From Peter Lindbergh to Timothy Greenfield-Sanders or Pierre Boucher, using enigmatic black-and-white photos, there has always been a timeless quality to all these covers.

Number three: Lui, the French men's magazine. In the 1970s, almost all the covers of Lui were extremely striking in their simplicity and effectiveness. From Romy Schneider's Christmas bottom to Brigitte Bardot as the official French Marianne or Catherine Deneuve in red pantyhose, these covers are simple and straight to the point—as the magazine's subject matter would require—yet very cleverly executed.

What is the key to art directing a magazine?
A massive Rolodex, the ability to sustain a strong vision in the long run, the know-how to create visual, conceptual, and emotional links between stories.

Which magazine would you most like to art direct?
Mostly I would like to art direct a one-off special edition of the American Vogue. Even if the Italian, British, and French Vogues are creatively superior, Vogue still remains the ultimate reference. I would love to art direct a single issue of this magazine and hopefully make it radical and absolute.

What inspires your creativity?
Everything. Sometimes I am concerned that my inspiration will dry up, but as soon as a client comes to me with a problem to resolve, ideas start to flow like water from a faucet. There is nothing more exciting to me than solving problems. I am a problem solver!

How much creative freedom were you given by the Big publishers, and how important is it to be given that?
I was fortunate enough to be given 100 percent carte blanche by the publishers: total control on the creative choices of the issue. Considering that Big magazine is almost solely an image-driven publication, if they were not to give total creative freedom to the art director it would be the equivalent of shooting themselves in the foot. The magazine can only live up to the enthusiasm of the art director who designs it.

Many famous and well-respected designers and art directors have put their mark on Big—obviously including yourself—but did this add pressure?
Yes and no. Yes, there was some pressure because you know that your peers and competitors will automatically take a look at it; and no, it did not really bother me because I did not design the magazine to show off, but rather as something I would enjoy if I were the reader.

How did you approach the project?
I approached it as a dream project, since that's the process that has always worked best for me. What would be the magazine I would be dying to put my hands and eyes on? Who would I love to see interpret my creative brief and directions?

Who did you work with to create it?
Spike Jonze, Roman Coppola, Mike Mills, Todd Cole, Dewey Nicks, Janice Dickinson, Charles Bukowski, Juliana Sohn, Paul Jasmin, Frank Gehry, Max Vadukul, Florian Maier-Aichen, Anette Aurell, Paul Ritter, Matthias Vriens, Arthur Mount, Mitchell Feinberg, George Stoll, Max Bean, Gregory Poe, Patrice Meigneux, Steven Lippman, Alix Lambert, Guillaume Wolf, Francesco Vezzoli, Nicoletta Munroe, Albert Giordan. From up-and-coming photographers and artists to established or even legendary writers and celebrities, my hope was that this strange and eclectic mix of human beings and talents would exhaust every minute aspect of Los Angeles.

What is important about the team that you work with on all your projects?
Teams change and are adapted to every project. In this case, it was less a team than a dream list of collaboration.

How important do you think the cover image on a magazine is?
The cover makes half of the magazine's impact. A bad cover is barely noticeable, diluted in the crowd of other publications at a newsstand; a good cover jumps out at you. A cover should obviously also sustain a certain longevity.

How did you decide on the one you chose for the LA issue of Big, and who was the photographer?
First, what I really didn't want was to "print" the name of the issue on the cover using typography, but rather for it to be embedded in the cover. So I came up with the idea of the pendant. I went to Downtown Los Angeles in the jewelry district and found a genial Armenian guy named Sirius, who, following my blueprint, executed the 24K gold VIP text-based necklace. Additionally, I had this obsession about exploring clichés. One of these was the cult of the body and a certain tackiness—which I happen not to dislike—that is very Los Angeles. I envisioned a man, an imaginary Heffner or Bob Evans, emerging from his pool. He's really too tan, all sweaty and greasy. He couldn't be hairless because this was not about perfection or showing an Adonis, but rather about building an epidermic and visceral feeling for the cover. In the end, I commissioned my longtime friend and collaborator Albert Giordan to shoot the photo. At the time of the shoot, we didn't have any budget left for a model, so I volunteered. Detractors can always look at it as a narcissistic choice, and in a sense it was, but I was really basking in—and must say still savor—the irony of the art director "making" the cover of the magazine.

If you had a chance to create your own magazine, what would it be?
I hope I will never listen to the sirens of the publishing world. Not that art directors have never been successful at creating their own dream magazine, but in the end, the truth is that most of the small- or medium-sized independent publications end up recreating exactly what they were trying to avoid in the first place. If, one day, I end up taking the plunge, I hope I will do it with strong logistical and financial backup, but most of all with the lucidity that this is not a fantasy job.

03

"Independent Web sites are the future in magazine publishing. The traffic that can be generated is beginning to far exceed the circulation of even the biggest titles."

Tom Hingston, Art Director, Stand Off

Format & Structure

"A good cover corresponds with the rest of the magazine. There is nothing more disappointing than buying a magazine because of its striking cover and finding out that the rest of the content and design cannot keep up with it."

Ralf Herms, Publisher and Art Director, +rosebud

Introduction

Although most magazines are published in A4 format (8¼ x 11¾in; 210 x 297mm), many publishers are breaking the mold and printing their titles in a number of different sizes. For evidence of this you only have to look at the magazine shelves in a bookstore and you will see the extraordinary variety of shapes and sizes in which magazines are published today: there is the larger format, London-based Tank magazine, for example; the smaller format, such as the US oneonenine magazine; or a whole range of formats, like Swiss title +rosebud. A magazine's format not only distinguishes it from other publications, but also adds another dimension to its design and character.

Inside a magazine, other areas that await the designer include pagination, advertising, typography, photography and illustration, and captions and credits. Pagination, or page planning, gives the magazine pace and flow and is key to making sure that each issue feels like a complete whole. The order in which articles appear has to fit around other considerations, such as advertising or regular columns and features, but this can lead to some experimental and unusual production and design techniques, as shown in this chapter.

There are also certain practical aspects of a magazine that the designer or art director must always take into account. Credits and captions are elements that need to be addressed, as they must be both accurate and functional, so a system has to be devised that makes clear which captions and credits go with what images. Another, often more experimental element, is typography. As with all information design, the key to good typography is successful communication: it should be clear, but at the same time needs to be interesting, engaging, and suited to the subject or theme.

Finally, it is the illustrations and photography that for many offer the most visually pleasing and stimulating aspect of magazine design. This chapter—and, indeed, this book—shows some great examples of innovative and inspiring use of both these disciplines. For some years now, the art of illustration has been having something of a revival, particularly within magazine publishing, but photography and photographers maintain their position, providing striking, creative, and memorable imagery within the pages of the countless magazines available.

Art Direction: **3 Deep Design**
Publisher: **Poster Australasia Pty Ltd**
Country: **Australia**

Poster magazine

Poster magazine, a quarterly magazine produced in Australia, features fashion, art, architecture, and design from Australia and is aimed at creative professionals in fashion, the arts, and design. Since its inception in 2001 it has evolved to become what is best described as a forum for the discussion, presentation, and critique of Australian culture. Each edition of Poster reflects emerging and established creative thinking by responding, through text and imagery, to a defined editorial theme.

3 Deep Design's brief for the issues shown here was to bring the editorial theme of each issue to life and present an engaging editorial experience. They did that through strong design and imagery, and especially through their use of typography. Each display typeface is original, created for Poster by 3 Deep Design.

"To benefit the theme of each issue of Poster and to be sympathetic to the overall narrative, flow, and feel of the magazine, we created new typefaces. It can never be a 'one shoe fits all' scenario for Poster as this would kill its very spirit and position," explained Principal Brett Phillips.

The theme for Issue 10 was codes of youth culture. As shown here, the cover features a stunning image by French photographer Jean-François Campos. The image is complemented by a great sense of activity and play between the typography, supporting grid and graphics, and the characters within the image. "It worked well to introduce the theme of the issue and as this cover shows, we also enjoy the fact that we continue not to work with a conventional masthead. People who follow Poster like to be inspired," says Phillips.

Art Direction: **Justin Kay**
Publisher: **Keith Denerstein**
Country: **USA**

Flo

American magazine Flo is aimed at teenage males, and the issue shown here—Volume 9—was the Back to School issue from 2005. Designed and art directed by New York designer Justin Kay, the issue features imagery from typical high school settings on the cover and throughout, including stickers, student lockers, and school notebook paper.

Kay describes Flo as being almost like an oversized CD booklet, as the magazine comes complete with free DVD and CD. Design is busy and "maximal," and layouts are unconventional and bold, with images to match—it works well in this context and for the intended audience. Illustrators featured in this issue are Steve Green and Max Vogel. Agbuch typeface has been used for all body copy, Container for the headline text, and many different typefaces for story-specific headline treatments.

Who will survive and what will they be wearing?
(L to R): On Monique: hat & sweater by Burton, t-shirt by Matix, thermal and jeans by Billabong. On Adrian: t-shirt & belt by 55DSL, sunglasses by Oakley, jeans by Matix, shoes by Draven
(L to R): On Adrian: sunglasses by Oakley, sweater by Burton, t-shirt by Matix, skirt by 55DSL, shoes by Draven. On Monique: sunglasses by Smith, jacket & jeans by Matix, t-shirt & backpack by 55DSL, belt by Burton
On Ashley: jacket & t-shirt by Matix, sunglasses by Smith
America's most stunning and hip fashion!....
"THE FLO STYLE CHAINSAW MASSACRE"
What happened is true. Now the fashion that's just as real.
Photos by David Yarovesky • Styled by Laila Wehbe and Kiersten Bryant
Make up by Clare Bendandi

BLACK BOOK
RAZA
BROOKLYN
MANHATTAN
BRONX QUEENS
STATEN ISLAND
N.Y.C
flo 58
Max Vogel
BLACK BOOK
Strife
Steve Green
59 flo

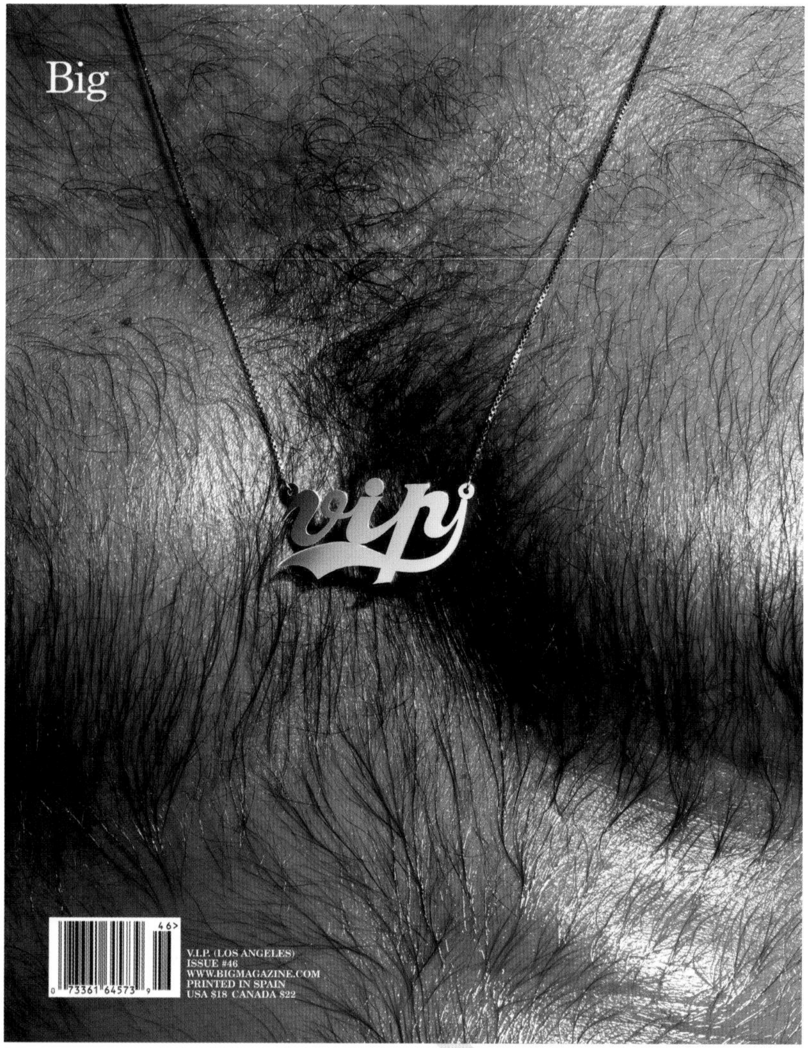

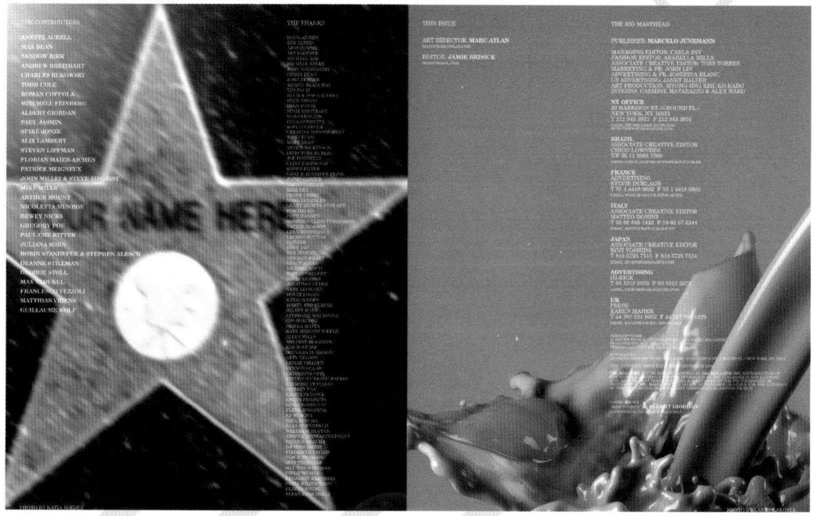

Art Direction: **Marc Atlan**
Publisher: **Big Magazine, Inc.**
Country: **USA**

Big, Los Angeles VIP special

When Marc Atlan was approached by the publishers of the prestigious Big magazine to art direct an issue, he was simply told to create an issue that gave his vision of his home city, Los Angeles. With LA being so vast and culturally diverse, Atlan was faced with many possible approaches. He began by creating a list of the elements, stories, and people he wanted to include in order to document different facets of the city.

Titled VIP, Atlan worked with many people to create the contents, including Spike Jonze, Roman Coppola, Charles Bukowski, Juliana Sohn, Frank Gehry, and Albert Giordan, who shot the cover image. The content is rich, and, like all issues of Big, it is image driven. Each spread has its own title, so, for example, one spread featuring photographs of a chambermaid at the Chateau Marmont is called "The Saint;" a city janitor in charge of cleaning the Walk of Fame stars is dubbed "The Perfectionist;" and a toothy Tom Cruise is "The One."

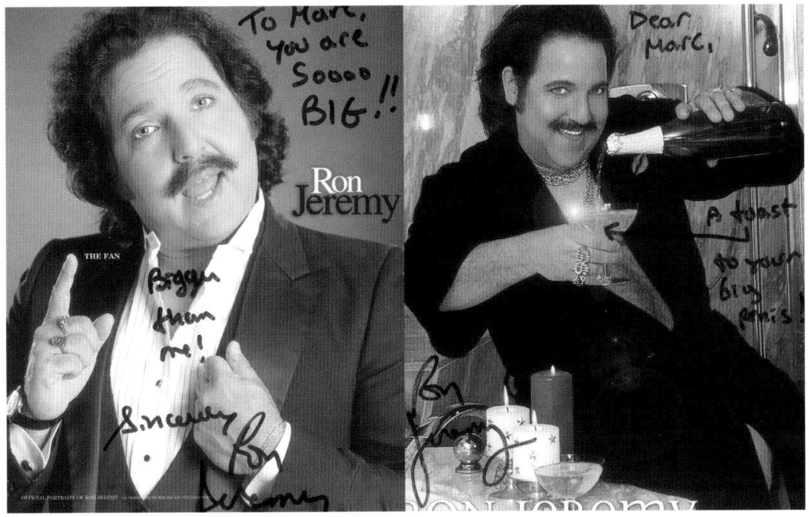

Typography in this issue was meant principally as discreet and generic titling. One typeface was chosen—Century Schoolbook—for its relative roundness, obvious sturdiness, and the clarity of its framework. It also happens that this typeface was originally cut at the beginning of the 20th century by Linn Boyd Benton—the father of famed typographer Morris Fuller Benton—specifically for the US magazine, Century Magazine. The schoolbook version of Century was later developed by American Type Founders in order to ensure maximum legibility for elementary school textbooks. Atlan saw it as a perfect fit for the purposes of the issue, designed as a "manual" to the city.

Atlan spent nine months conceiving, art directing, and designing this special issue. "The best thing about working on this project was to tackle such a vast, complex, and contradictory subject as Los Angeles," he explains. "I sincerely believe this issue is rich visually, in content, and in ideas, and I think people are intrigued by it."

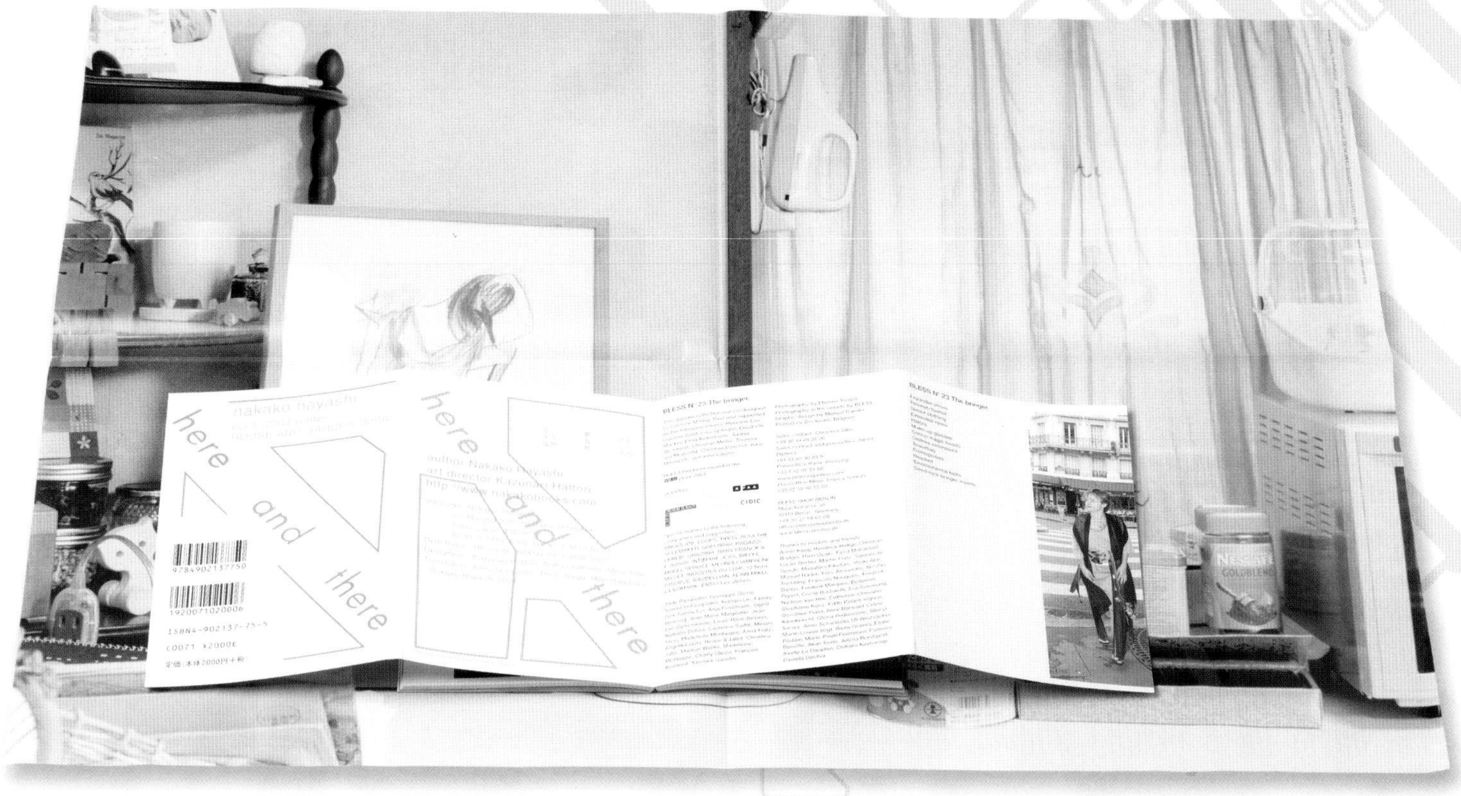

Art Direction: **Kazunari Hattori**
Editor: **Nakako Hayashi**
Publisher: **Nakako Hayashi**
Country: **Japan**

here and there

Japanese magazine here and there is a reflection of Editor and Publisher Nakako Hayashi's life. It is inspired by the people around her and the things she sees each day. "No other magazines were talking about the people or the things I believed to be important at the time, so I started up a magazine," explains Hayashi. "I had worked as an editor for a monthly fashion magazine for 13 years, but wanted to stop being an anonymous tastemaker and instead, speak in my own voice."

In 2006 here and there reached its fifth issue, and it has featured interviews with fashion designers, including Bless, Susan Cianciolo, and Cosmic Wonder, as well as artists such as Mark Borthwick. Issue 5 itself—shown here—was dedicated to the house and garden. Takashi Homma photographed his Brooklyn garden and shot images of Hayashi's flat, and Hayashi herself photographed and wrote about the Kyoto Gardens. The magazine has been printed in a small, postcard-size format, divided into two sections by fold-out flaps, making a compact magazine with a personal feel appropriate to the subject matter.

here
nakako hayashi
here and there
2002 autumn issue
GALLERY 360°

Art Direction: **Ani Watanabe for GeneveTokyo**
Publisher: **GeneveTokyo**
Country: **Japan**

GeneveTokyo

GeneveTokyo is a small, but perfectly formed magazine produced in Tokyo by Yoko Sato and Ani Watanabe. It is all about culture and art, and, by featuring short interviews, profiles, and images of their work, it aims to introduce young creatives and artists to the world, such as T-shirt artist Masafumi Sanai, artist Masakatsu Shimoda, and Swiss graphic designers Büro Destruct.

GeneveTokyo does not have the usual magazine format. It is simply made from one sheet of paper that has been folded to make 16 pages of the magazine. The art direction and design follows on from this with simple, clean layouts, a subtle color palette, and the use of Helvetica and Univers typefaces. It is produced independently and features no advertising, but is slowly being distributed in more and more markets, including Europe and the USA.

WE TRAVEL FAST [CHONGKING]
WE TRAVEL FAR [BORO DESTRUCT]
WWW.BORODESTRUCT.NET

Art Direction: **Masoud Golsorkhi**
Publisher: **Tank Publications Ltd**
Country: **UK**

Tank

Tank was founded in 1998 by Iranian-born photographer Masoud Golsorkhi and German art director Andreas Laüfer. It was one of the first of its kind, with an innovative format and unusual mix of content. Original design, high-end production values, and contributions by and collaborations with some of the best and most cutting-edge creatives has kept Tank at the very top of the magazine market and launched the careers of many new talents.

It is perhaps the design brief—make flicking through the magazine the equivalent of the experience of flicking through record covers at a record shop—that keeps Tank's design fresh and innovative. It has a fast-paced front section of smaller features followed by longer features on art, movies, music, architecture, and literature.

Over the years Tank has worked with photographers such as Stefano Galuzzi, Sean and Seng, Ali Madhavi, and Katherine Wolkoff, and has been so successful that brands have approached the publishers to collaborate on other publications as well as advertising campaigns and packaging design. In 2000 they published MINED, which spells "denim" backward, for Levi's, which won them a D&AD award, and subsequently developed advertising campaigns for Christian Lacroix, perfume-packaging design for Giorgio Armani and Jean Paul Gaultier Perfumes, and magazines for Liberty and Swarovski.

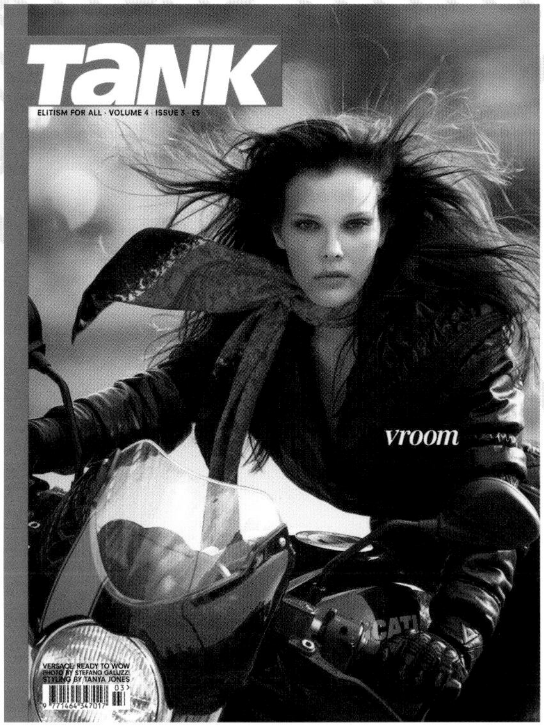

TANK
ELITISM FOR ALL · VOLUME 4 · ISSUE 3 · £5
vroom
VERSACE: READY TO WOW
PHOTO BY STEFANO GALUZZI
STYLING BY TANYA JONES

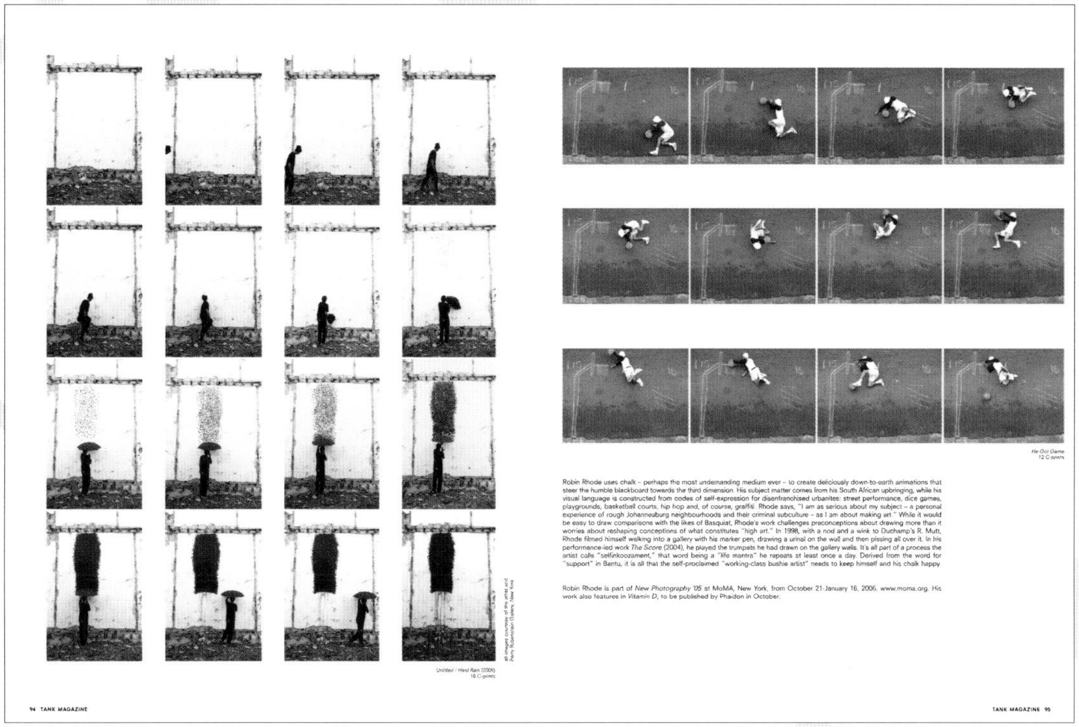

Robin Rhode uses chalk – perhaps the most undemanding medium ever – to create deliciously down-to-earth animations that steer the humble blackboard towards the third dimension. His subject matter comes from his South African upbringing, while his visual language is constructed from codes of self-expression for disenfranchised urbanites: street performance, dice games, playgrounds, basketball courts, hip hop and, of course, graffiti. Rhode says, "I am as serious about my subject – a personal experience of rough Johannesburg neighbourhoods and their criminal subculture – as I am about making art." While it would be easy to draw comparisons with the likes of Basquiat, Rhode's work challenges preconceptions about drawing more than it worries about reshaping conceptions of what constitutes "high art." In 1998, with a nod and a wink to Duchamp's R. Mutt, Rhode filmed himself walking into a gallery with his marker pen, drawing a urinal on the wall and then pissing all over it. In his performance-led work *The Score* (2004), he played the trumpets he had drawn on the gallery walls. It's all part of a process the artist calls "selfinkoozament," that word being a "life mantra" he repeats at least once a day. Derived from the word for "support" in Bantu, it is all that the self-proclaimed "working-class bushie artist" needs to keep himself and his chalk happy

Robin Rhode is part of *New Photography '05* at MoMA, New York, from October 21-January 16, 2006. www.moma.org. His work also features in *Vitamin D*, to be published by Phaidon in October.

94 TANK MAGAZINE

TANK MAGAZINE 95

REMEMBRANCE
OF THINGS PAST
PHOTOGRAPHY BY STEFANO GALUZZI · STYLING BY PATTI WILSON

Art Direction: **Saturday**
Publisher: **Condé Nast**
Country: **UK**

GQ Style

GQ Style is a men's fashion biannual. Its aim is to be the essential guide to what to wear each season, but it also covers what is happening in art, design, and architecture. Saturday was commissioned to design each issue. The magazine keeps the same sections each season, but has a different theme that is interpreted in a new way each time. The brief as such was simple: to create a design that is utterly contemporary yet still in the aspirational world of Condé Nast publications such as Vogue.

Shown here is the first issue designed by Saturday. The theme was Work, and this is reflected not just in the design, but also in the art direction. The art directors collaborated with many people, from such legends as Nick Knight and Peter Lindbergh to provocateurs like Terry Richardson, to artists Tom Hunter and Andreas Gursky. A custom-made typeface that embodies the "masculine" ideals of work was used.

Shown here is the opening spread, called "Terry's Hombres," which is a good example of typography and image working together. The designers took a part of the image and filled the letters with it, giving it a modern feel that is relevant to the story as well as emphasizing the headline's purpose.

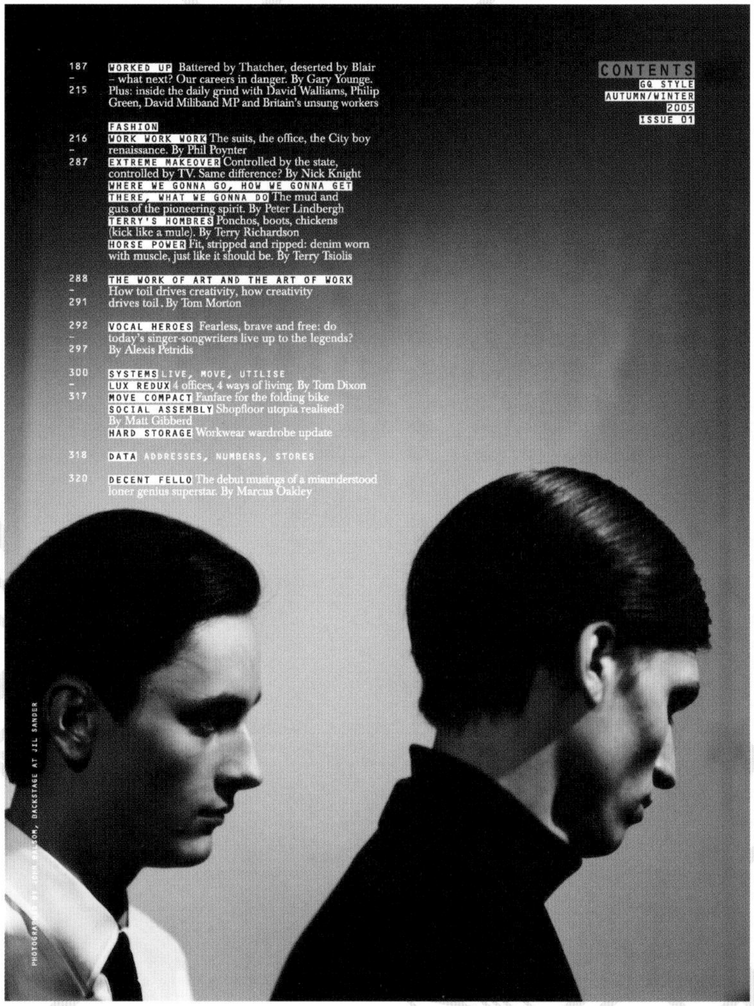

TERRY'S
HOMBRES
By TERRY RICHARDSON

WHERE
WE
GONNA GO
HOW
WE
GONNA
GET
THERE
WHAT
WE
GONNA
DO
By PETER LINDBERGH

Art Direction: **Phil Evans/Rob Kester**
Publisher: **Foto8 Ltd**
Country: **UK**

EI8HT

EI8HT is a quarterly magazine aimed at photojournalists and photo editors. When briefed on its design, Art Directors Phil Evans and Rob Kester were asked to create a "look" for the magazine that was credible and grounded as well as visually arresting, without detracting from the content.

After discussions, they decided to reduce the number of design elements used and created a magazine using only the minimum number of items. The nature of the publication means that the designers always get to work with images that are of the highest quality, giving both the covers and inside spreads real visual strength.

An Avant Garde "8" is used as the masthead, with Helvetica employed for all the text-page typography. The design of EI8HT exemplifies the power of both imagery and typography. "We wanted the layout to be intense and intoxicating," explain the designers. "Graphically we left very little white space, to create a claustrophobic feel."

Eyes Wide Open

Andrew Tasta left the Balkans for a working trip to the Surin islands off the coast of Thailand to photograph the Moken, nomadic Sea Gypsies who spend eight months of the year at sea. A month later, the tsunami struck, and although the Moken lost their homes, ancestral wisdom saved their lives. Whether it can save their way of life remains to be seen
Eyes Wide Open
Once upon a time among the most beautiful islands in the world lived the Sea Gypsies. During the winter months they built bamboo houses on the water's edge and lived happily, isolated from the rest of the world by the powerful ocean. In the long, hot summer, they would fashion boats and spend the season at sea.

Jonas and the Cherries

Art Direction: **Dario Utreras/Jeff Cochrane/Fernando del Villar**
Publisher: **Bulb Media Ltd.**
Country: **UK**

Bulb

Bulb, a global-issues magazine aimed at youth, addresses matters ranging from trade justice, human rights, and the environment to conflict, race, migration, health, and corporate power. This is mixed with the latest in music, sport, fashion, and culture from the global underground, all of which is written and illustrated by young people from around the world.

"The seeds of Bulb were planted while I was working in Latin America as a market researcher for Levi's," explains Editor Amaranta Wright. "I began to think, if only the thoughts and feelings I was collecting from young people could be used to encourage their visions for a fairer and more peaceful world rather than be manipulated to steer them toward consuming things."

Back in Britain, Wright started Bulb to reflect and feed the values of justice and peace, tolerance, and solidarity that most young people themselves desire, but which are ignored by the mainstream media. The aim of Bulb is to encourage this youth sector in their campaigning for peace, human rights, and social justice, and broaden awareness of these issues among the wider youth audience.

The idea behind the design of the magazine is to get away from the "lifestyle" or "consumer" approach to everything, and instead produce a product that reflected the authenticity and very real idealism of the content. As designer Dario Utreras explains: "We wanted to let the content speak for itself, for our young readers to be challenged, motivated, and inspired by it, but also we wanted the content to be clearly understood and not be too serious."

To that end, Utreras and his team have found a balance between existing teen-pop magazine culture and the more serious, logical, analytical design often used in politics-oriented magazines and newspapers. By mixing references from both of these worlds they have created something their readers can understand clearly and at the same time be intrigued by.

"We work with artists, illustrators, and photographers on a collaborative basis," adds Utreras. "Young students or graduates, known and not so known, inspiring talent from different backgrounds, all of whom are actively interested in and concerned with global issues raised in the magazine. Their contribution is incredibly important."

Initially targeting a 15 to 19 age group, Bulb has now widened its readership to 14 to 24, and has proved highly successful in filling what was a huge gap in the market. Its energy comes from the participation of young people both in editorial and design, but it is balanced by the contributions of more established columnists.

SOILED FASHION

It is not just our food and booze that has gone down the organic route, clothes have also started to take a healthier and chemically-free turn. This month we show a small selection of the organic clothes on offer, perfect for getting down and dirty this autumn.

Photography: jenny Nordquist
www.jennynordquist.com

Styling: Amie H
www.amie_622@yahoo.co.uk.com

Hair & Make up: Mobeen
mobeenfarooq@hotmail.com

Models:
Bayley Freer
Vladimir Laurentiev
Alan

The current consumer interest in organic food has now led to the expansion of other areas of the organic industry including cotton farming. Cotton is often mistaken as a clean and environmentally friendly crop, in fact, cotton is the biggest user of insecticides in the world and many are greatly used in the developing countries. Conventionally farmed cotton is responsible for using nearly a quarter of the world's insecticides and over ten per cent of all pesticides. It is these pesticides that are damaging the ecology of surrounding areas, killing wildlife- mainly birds and fish, polluting the soil and poisoning water systems. A conventional cotton farmer would also use three thousand cubic metres more water per acre than an organic cotton farmer.
Using these expensive chemicals is not only hazardous towards our environment, but they endanger the health and safety of cotton farmers and their workers too. In the developing world three million people suffer from the affects of pesticide poisoning each year and twenty thousand consequently die. Organic cotton is grown without the use of synthetic pesticides and fertilisers, as well as genetically modified organisms and like other organic products, is healthier for the earth and its inhabitants. Ordinary cotton has a very similar appearance to organic cotton but when you compare the two, organic cotton is generally whiter and much shinier. It is also softer that conventional cotton and wears well over a long period of time. Farmers who have converted to organic cotton growing have improved their income by cutting the cost of inputs and accessing a premium for certified organic crops

Stephanie Hoyle

bulb
Bright Ideas from Underground
Issue 5
THE PRICE OF RESISTANCE
WHAT WILL YOU PAY FOR CHANGE?
PLUS
BECK EXCLUSIVE/ JOHN PILGER/ AFRICA'S KILLER COLTAN/MUSIC'S REAL CONSCIOUS BANDS/ BENJAMIN ZEPHANIAH
ISSN 1744-7380 £2.50

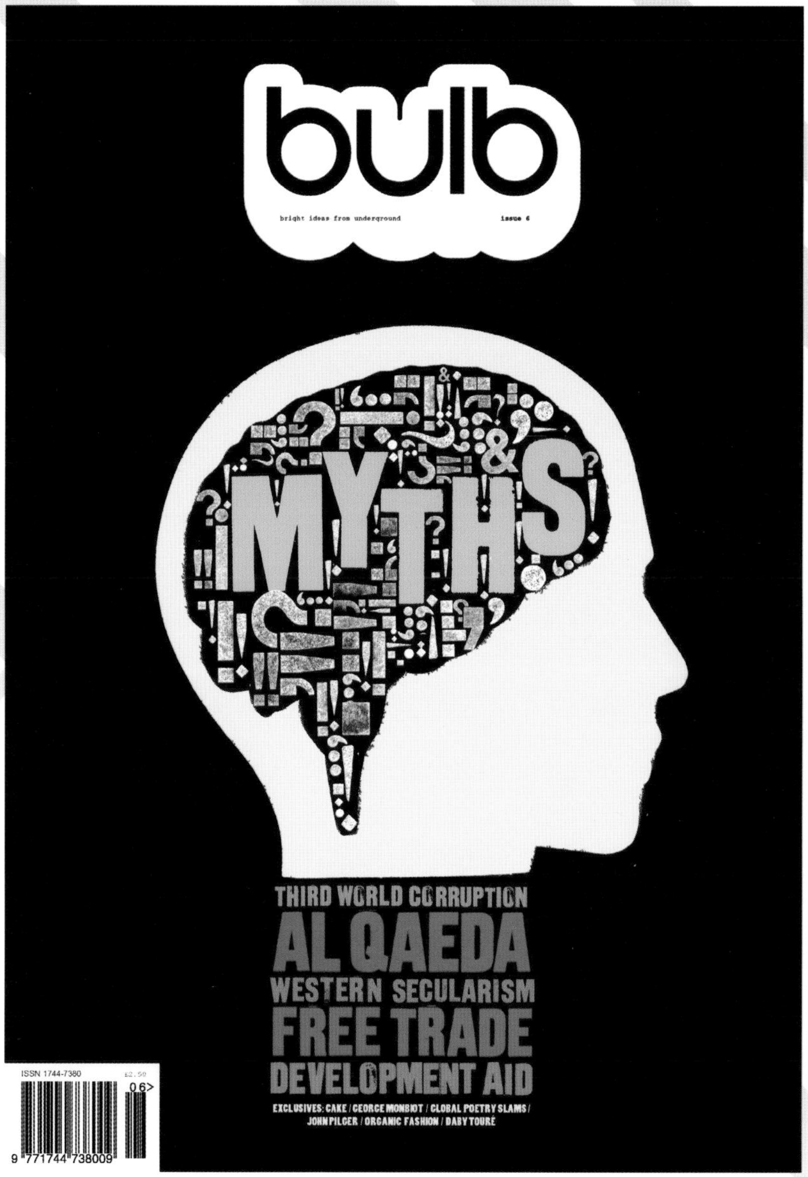
bulb
bright ideas from underground
issue 6
MYTHS
THIRD WORLD CORRUPTION
AL QAEDA
WESTERN SECULARISM
FREE TRADE
DEVELOPMENT AID
EXCLUSIVES: CAKE / GEORGE MONBIOT / GLOBAL POETRY SLAMS / JOHN PILGER / ORGANIC FASHION / DABY TOURÉ
ISSN 1744-7380

Art Direction: **Vier5**
Publisher: **Vier5**
Country: **France**

Fairy Tale

This is essentially a fashion magazine, but it reflects an unusual take on fashion and the world around it. Independently produced by Vier5 in Paris since 2002, Fairy Tale is a mix of strong, inspiring, often raw photography combined with unusual layout and design.

"We wanted to create a magazine that was based on the view of a designer and not of an editor," explains Marco Fiedler at Vier5. "Fairy Tale is like a documentary of our interests and people that we are interested in. This could be an interesting face, an interesting fashion designer, or perhaps an artist like Claus Richter or Lewis Baltz."

The designers work with their own typefaces and abandon all the usual rules for magazine design to create quite abstract layouts. Covers are often multiple and also screen printed—the first issue had more than 400 variations of cover color—but the inside is simply printed in black and white.

AUX CHEMINS DE FLEURS
TEL. 01.40.05.04.03

Art Direction: **Rob Crane/Martin Yates**
Publisher: **125 World Ltd.**
Country: **UK**

125

125 magazine, launched in 2003, acts as an "international image gallery" featuring the work of photographers and image-makers. It was started as a luxury publication to provide a space for both up-and-coming and established image-makers to express their creative ideas. The unique difference with 125 is that every image in the magazine can be bought as a large-format, limited-edition print—it is a gallery in which you can browse and from which you can buy.

Production values are high, with a gloss cover and quality stock used throughout. The design is simple and clean, allowing the work of each featured artist to breathe, and advertising is kept to a limit of no more than 10 percent of each issue, which makes it seem more like a book than a magazine. Featured artists include Nick Clements, Kent Baker, James Dimmock, Jason Joyce, Christopher Griffith, Rick Guest, Emma Hardy, Sam Perry, Jennifer Smit, and Perry Curties. An interesting concept, it is beautifully executed with each issue.

125
Love

Issue 06: Love

EMMA HARDY
ROAD

Art Direction: **Big Block Creative**
Publisher: **Independent**
Country: **Australia**

Sneaker Freaker

Sneaker Freaker is, as the title suggests, all about sneakers. Published in Melbourne, Australia, it is the first and only international sneaker magazine to document the modern footwear craze as a global phenomenon. It is produced biannually, and features articles written by "sneaker freaks" from around the world, with shopping guides to all the major cities, interviews with designers and collectors, news on new releases, opinion pieces, store reports, and detailed overviews of brand heritage.

Published in 2002, the first issue has become something of a cult collectors' item, selling for a small fortune on eBay. As founder Woody has said: "I wanted it to be the best fanzine about sneakers ever made." With that in mind, Sneaker Freaker is fanzine size—A5 (5¾ x 8¼in/148 x 210mm)—but with much higher production values. It is printed on uncoated stock, and each page is full to bursting with either text or images.

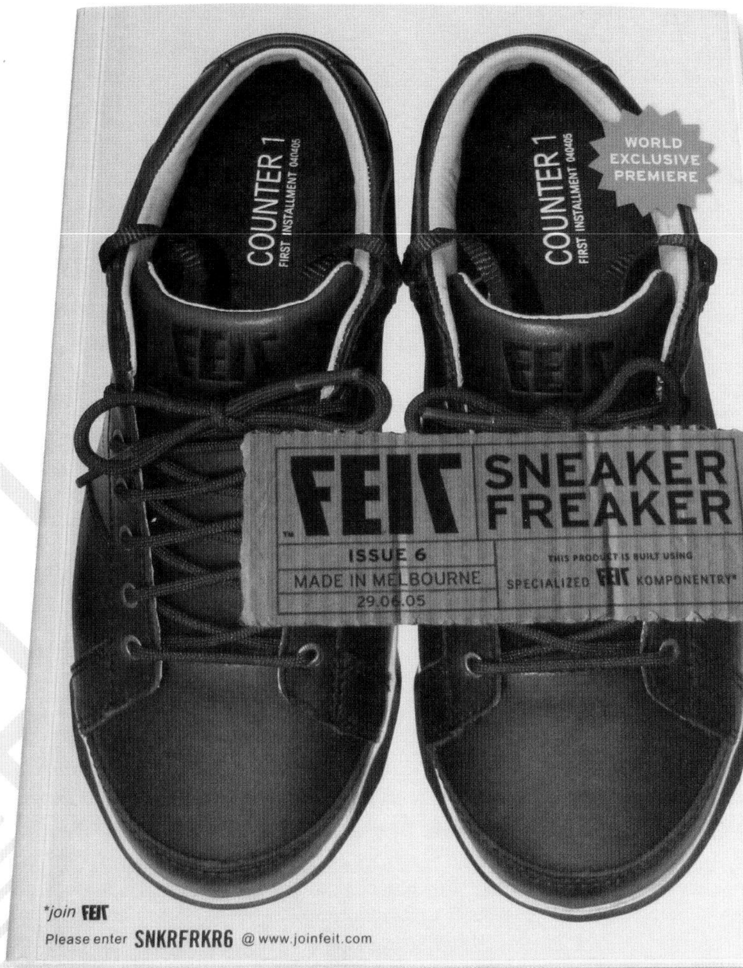

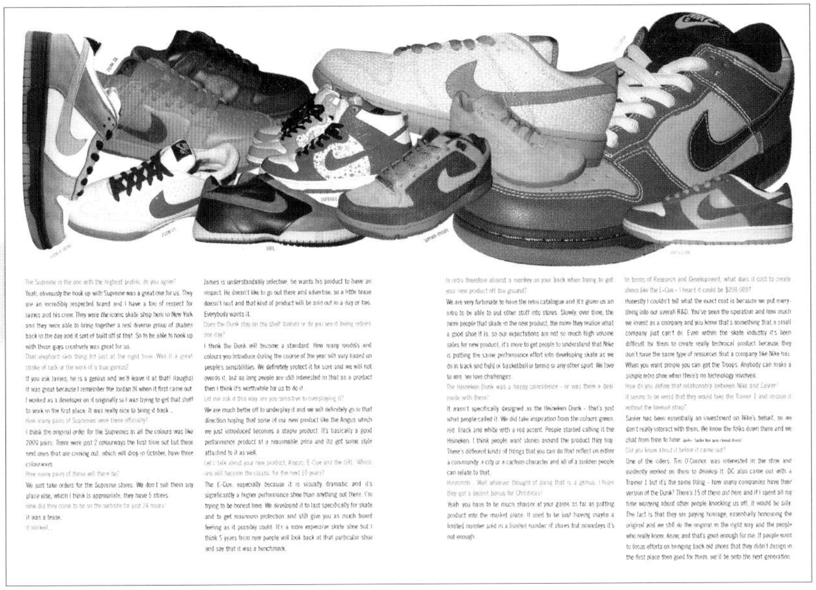

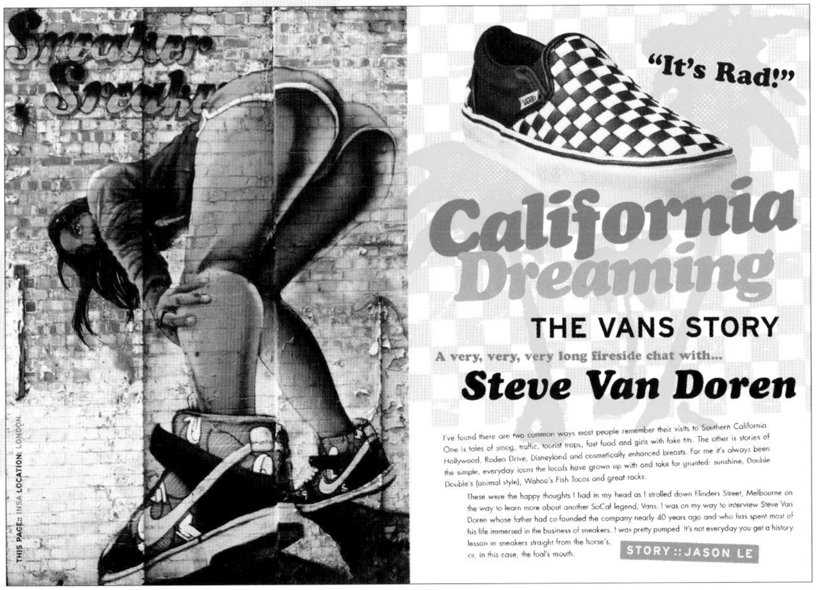

"It's Rad!"
California Dreaming
THE VANS STORY
A very, very, very long fireside chat with...
Steve Van Doren
I've found there are two common ways most people remember their visits to Southern California. One is tales of smog, traffic, tourist traps, fast food and girls with fake tits. The other is stories of Hollywood, Rodeo Drive, Disneyland and cosmetically enhanced breasts. For me it's always been the simple, everyday icons the locals have grown up with and take for granted: sunshine, Double Double's (animal style), Wahoo's Fish Tacos and great racks.
These were the happy thoughts I had in my head as I strolled down Flinders Street, Melbourne on the way to learn more about another SoCal legend, Vans. I was on my way to interview Steve Van Doren whose father had co-founded the company nearly 40 years ago and who has spent most of his life immersed in the business of sneakers. I was pretty pumped. It's not everyday you get a history lesson in sneakers straight from the horse's, or, in this case, the foal's mouth.
STORY :: JASON LE

THIS PAGE:: INSA LOCATION: LONDON

Art Direction: **Eric Pillault/Antoine Jean**
Publisher: **Editions Jalou**
Country: **France**

Jalouse

Jalouse is France's leading women's fashion magazine, covering trends in fashion, culture, the arts, music, and movies. First published in 1997, it was created by the Jalou family, who wanted to put together a "young-thinking" magazine made by young, forward-thinking people—"women about town" aged between 20 and 35—that was at the time missing in the magazine market.

The design is simplistic, with a graphic approach, and many full-page images throughout each issue. Photographers featured include Matthew Frost, Luis Sanchis, Alan Clarke, Christophe Rihet, Benjamin Nitot, Jean-Baptiste Mondino, and Elina Kechicheva. The cover image shown here was shot by Jean-Baptiste Mondino; all other images by Luis Sanchis.

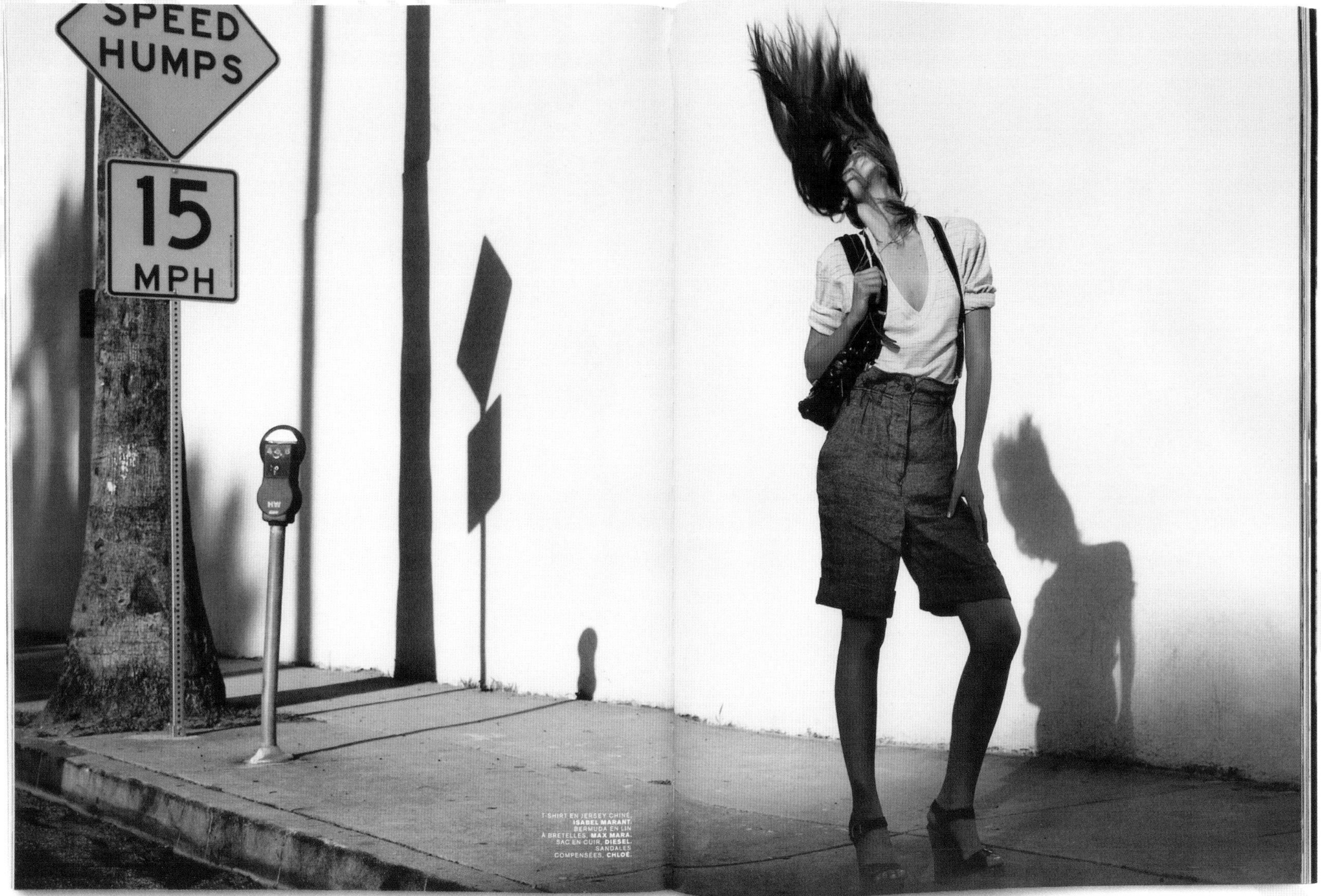
SPEED
HUMPS
15
MPH
T-SHIRT EN JERSEY CHINÉ,
ISABEL MARANT.
BERMUDA EN LIN
À BRETELLES, MAX MARA.
SAC EN CUIR, DIESEL.
SANDALES
COMPENSÉES, CHLOÉ.

Sara Forestier en enfer
Diane Kruger pète les plombs
Spécial Mode 100 pages de tendances et d'accessoires
Les agitateurs de la scène arty

Mannequins au bord de la crise de nerfs
Frankie – le top au bout du rouleau interprété par Diane Kruger* – n'est pas la seule à craquer. Depuis toujours, les mannequins de légende ont flirté avec la dépression

Le temple rock de New York

Arty pris
Nouveau focus ? L'art contemporain. Hier réservé aux initiés, il mobilise aujourd'hui autant les collectionneurs sérieux que les modeux. Panorama des acteurs et lieux de cette nouvelle scène

Art Direction: **Jonathan Barnbrook**
Design: **Barnbrook Design**
Publisher: **Hakuhodo**
Country: **Japan**

Kohkoku

Kohkoku is published by the second-biggest advertising agency in Japan, Hakuhodo. The word kohkoku means "advertising" in Japanese, and the magazine was originally published as an in-house agency magazine, but is now also to be found in various cultural bookstores in Japan.

Kohkoku had existed for a number of years before London-based designer Jonathan Barnbook was brought in as Designer and Art Director. The previous editor of the magazine knew of Barnbrook from the work he'd done for anticorporate title Adbusters.

Because of this, the editor wanted to make the magazine much more about changing attitudes and tackling social issues than sticking with the light, lifestyle content that had typified it up to that time.

"The idea the editor came up with was to reflect very strongly that the magazine was to do with social issues, so he wanted the 'red square,'as in the Russian Revolution, to be the starting point," explains Barnbrook. He and his team started by changing the format of the magazine to a square, and then followed the concept through in the rest of the design.

A new headline font, Coma, was designed and used throughout the magazine. The font's design is based on the square concept, so it could easily be used in conjunction with Japanese characters, which can be written either horizontally or vertically.

Barnbrook art directed six issues of this bimonthly title. For each issue, the editor commissioned a number of Japanese designers to lay out the different articles in the magazine while he and his team designed the front and back cover and the first eight pages.

The front cover always contained the word "let's" and then the subject of the issue. For example, Issue 1: Let's Exchange, published in 2001, dealt with the theme of meaningful interchange between people, while Issue 2: Let's Play, discussed issues concerning the environment. "With this project we wanted to create something that was visually new for each issue and to put over the different concept that each issue was focusing on," explains Barnbrook. "I had a lot of freedom, the editor knew my work, so knew the kind of designer they would be working with. Luckily the editor and I had similar ideological outlooks."

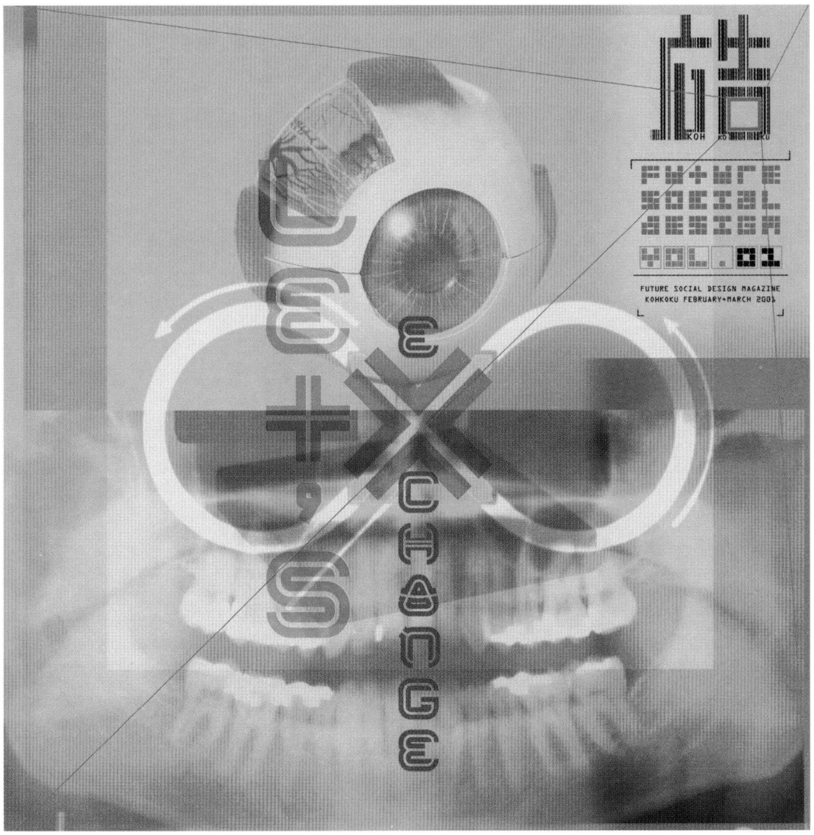

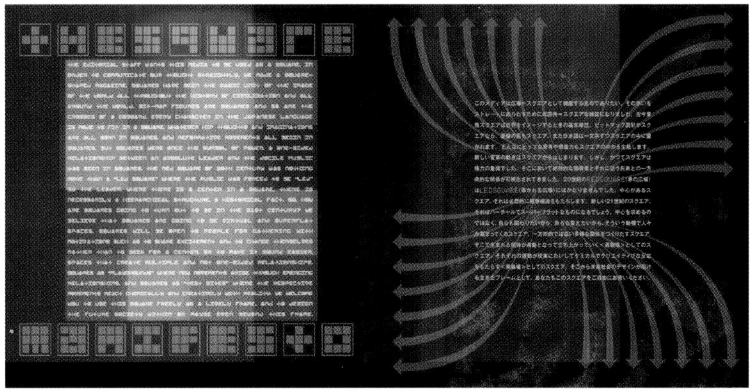

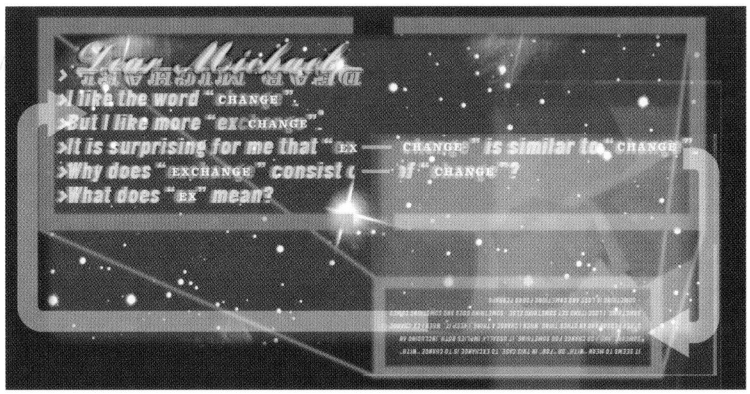

広告
FUTURE SOCIAL DESIGN MAGAZINE
LET'S
PLAY

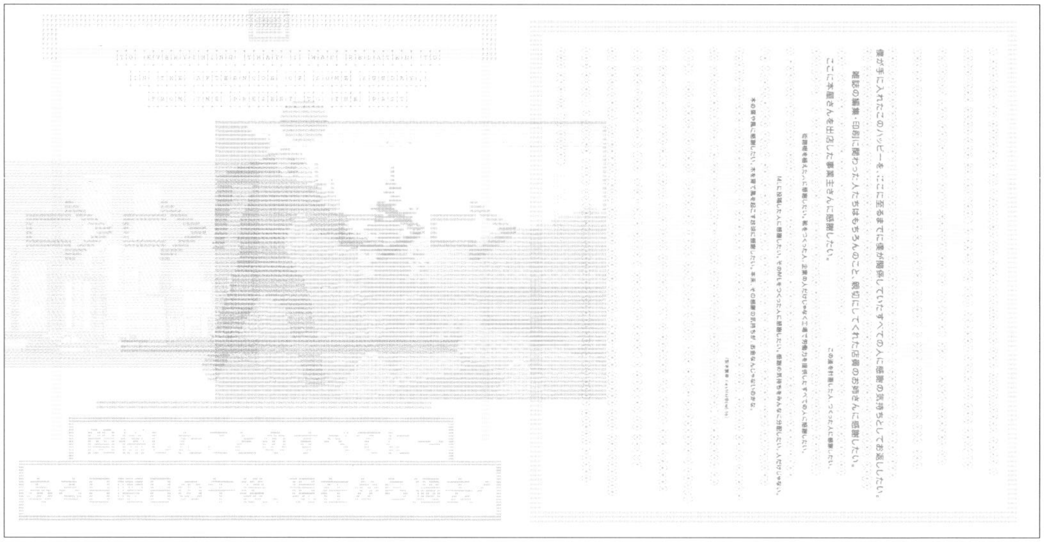
関係したことのすべてに〜
ある日曜日の午後、現在から過去へ

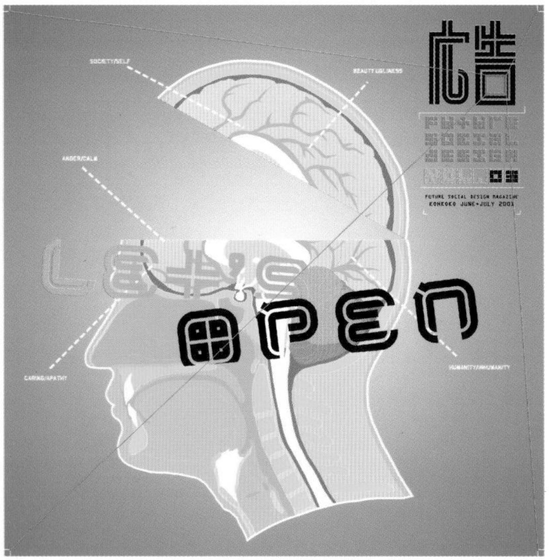
広告
FUTURE SOCIAL DESIGN MAGAZINE
LET'S
OPEN

GOVERNMENT IS A SACRED TRUST OF THE PEOPLE, THE AUTHORITY FOR WHICH IS DERIVED FROM THE PEOPLE, THE POWERS OF WHICH ARE EXERCISED BY THE REPRESENTATIVES OF THE PEOPLE, AND THE BENEFITS OF WHICH ARE ENJOYED BY THE PEOPLE. THIS IS A UNIVERSAL PRINCIPLE OF MANKIND UPON WHICH THIS CONSTITUTION IS FOUNDED. WE REJECT AND REVOKE ALL CONSTITUTIONS, LAWS, ORDINANCES, AND RESCRIPTS IN CONFLICT HEREWITH.
そもそも国政は、国民の厳粛な信託によるものであつて、その権威は国民に由来し、その権力は国民の代表者がこれを行使し、その福利は国民がこれを享受する。これは人類普遍の原理であり、この憲法は、かかる原理に基くものである。われらは、これに反する一切の憲法、法令及び詔勅を排除する。
WE
THE JAPANESE PEOPLE
日本国民は、
DESIRE PEACE
FOR ALL TIME
恒久の平和を念願し、
AND DEEPLY CONSCIOUS OF THE
HIGH IDEALS
人間相互の関係を支配する
CONTROLLING
崇高な理想を
深く自覚するのであつて、
HUMAN RELATIONSHIP,

広告
FUTURE
SOCIAL
DESIGN
VOL.04
LET'S
DESIGN

WHAT IS
GOOD
DESIGN?
EXCERPTS FROM THE
ESSAY
"THE END"
BY KARRIE JACOBS
AND
TIBOR KALMAN
Design has become the significant creative act of our day. Music isn't composed, it's designed. Movies aren't scripted, they are designed. Books aren't written, they are designed. Political views aren't formulated over a lifetime, they are designed.
The concern is style, not content.
大事なのは形式であって
中身ではない。

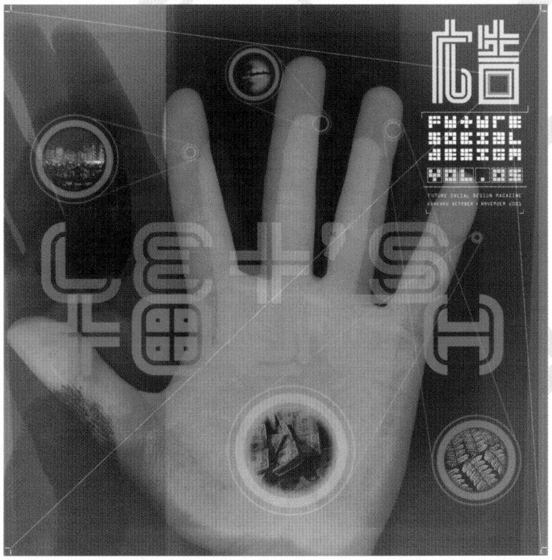
広告
FUTURE
SOCIAL
DESIGN
VOL.05
LET'S
TOUCH

TOUCH

TOUCH

Art Direction: **Honest**
Designer: **Honest**
Publisher: **Honest**
Country: **USA**

HONEST

HONEST magazine is described by its publishers as a handbook of creativity, a "how to" for visual minds, and a venue in which to display art, design, illustration, and photography. It was started as a way for the publishers—themselves designers—to showcase their own nonclient work as well as that of their creative friends.

"We love the process of taking a client's needs and problem-solving their issues to create great design, but we also enjoy total freedom and expressing ourselves without the limitation that can come with client work," explains Publisher and Art Director Jon Milott. "We thought others would enjoy and appreciate seeing our otherwise unpublished work, people similar to us who work in creative industries."

Between client projects they gathered content from their own work and that of their friends, and began the process of putting it all together to make Honest. It took a number of years, but the result is a stunningly bold, colorful, and uniquely designed publication. It features the work of photographers Corey Arnold and Mark Mahaney, and illustrations by Jim Woodring, Myron Macklin, and Amanda Behr.

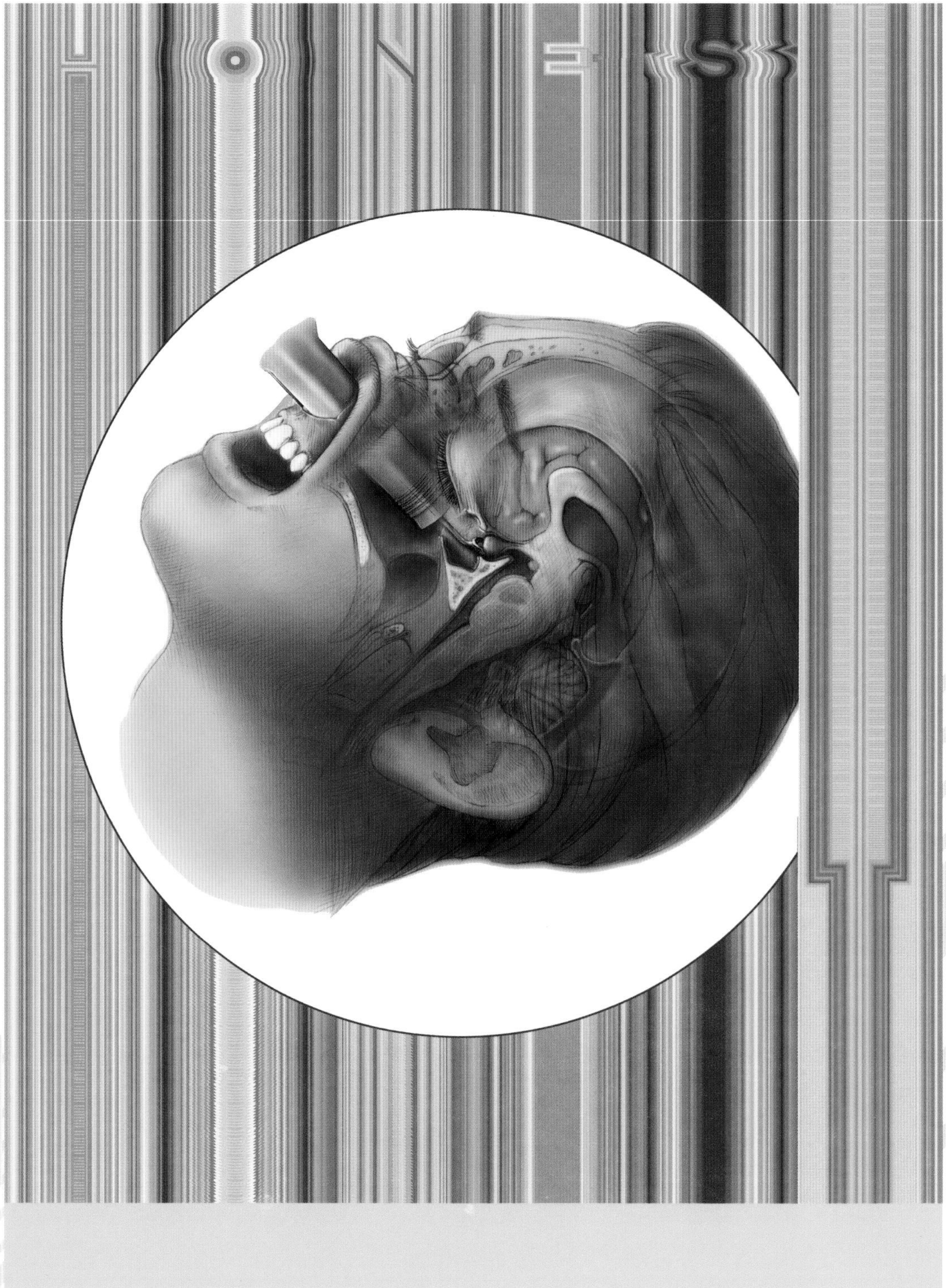

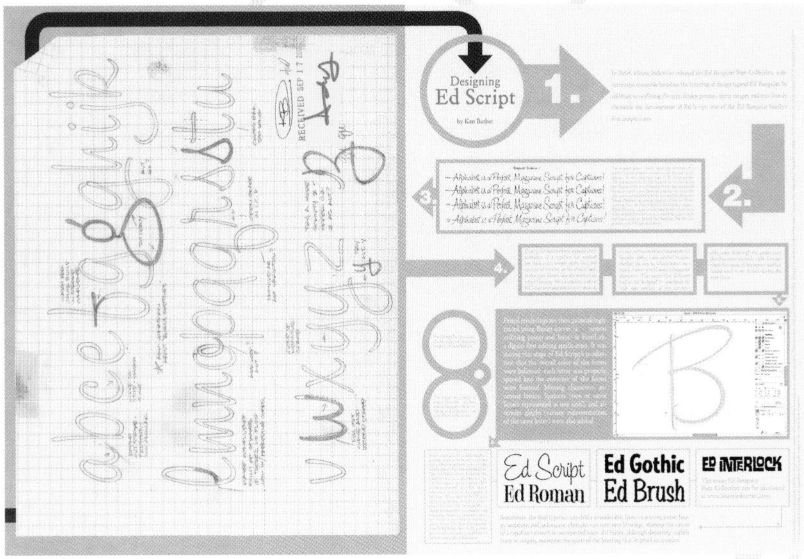
Designing
Ed Script
by Ken Barber
1.
2.
3.
4.
Ed Script
Ed Roman
Ed Gothic
Ed Brush
ED INTERLOCK

TYPES of SCIENCE FICTION
Space warfare

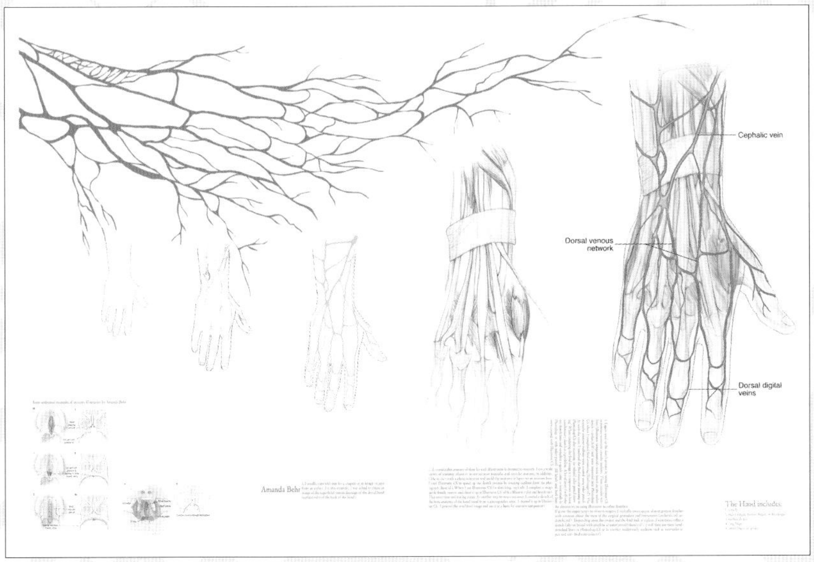
Cephalic vein
Dorsal venous
network
Dorsal digital
veins

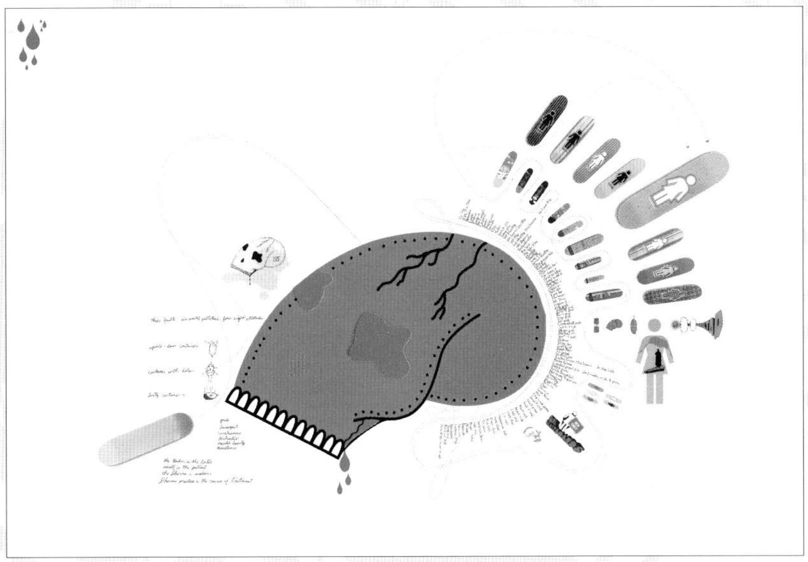

Art Direction: **Milos Jovanovic**
Publisher: **Stefan Cosma/Ioana Isopescu (Isoni Design)**
Country: **Romania**

Omagiu

Bucharest-based Omagiu magazine was launched in 2005. It is a concept magazine that aims to establish a common platform for different creative media—visual arts, music, fashion, and design—and promote young Romanian artists. Its founders felt that there was nothing in the market that was giving such artists the opportunity to showcase their work. "We saw that after around 2000 more and more creative independent projects popped up in Romania," explains Publisher Stefan Cosma, "it was our belief that a platform should be created to gather these projects under one umbrella. The intention of Omagiu is to be a springboard for different talented artists in Romania."

The name of the magazine means "homage," and was the word used by the Romanian dictator Ceausescu to describe his lifetime's work. Since then, in Romania the word is directly associated with the communist period. "By using this name for our magazine we wanted to try to somehow rebrand this word and use it to pay homage to people who really need wider public recognition," adds Cosma. The intention of inverting senses can also be seen in the magazine's logo, shown here.

Alexandra Croitoru, Camil Dumitrescu, and Stefan Cosma manage the photography, while Matei Branea, Marina Moldovan, Dan Miron, and Bottega Areté from Denmark were responsible for illustrations. Hoefler Text is used throughout the magazine for the body text—one of the few fonts with proper Unicode that is free—and Akkurat, ARS Robust, and Fig Script also feature.

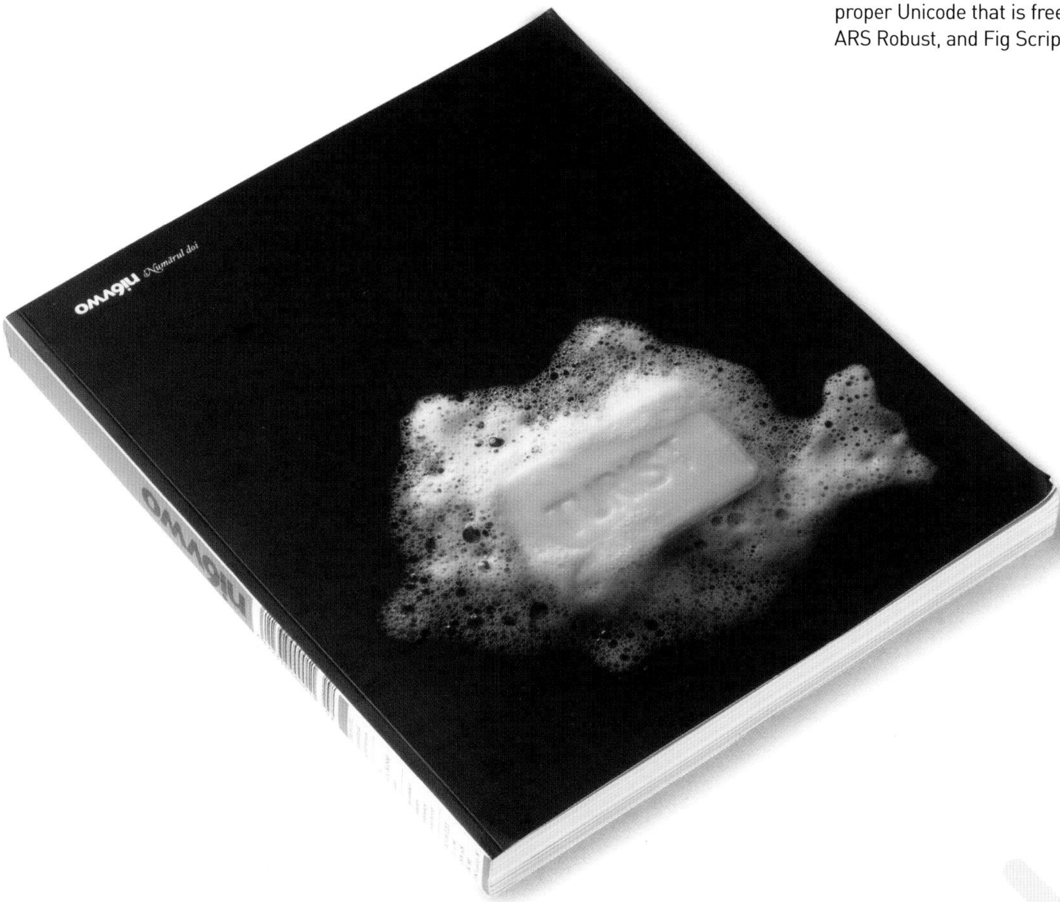

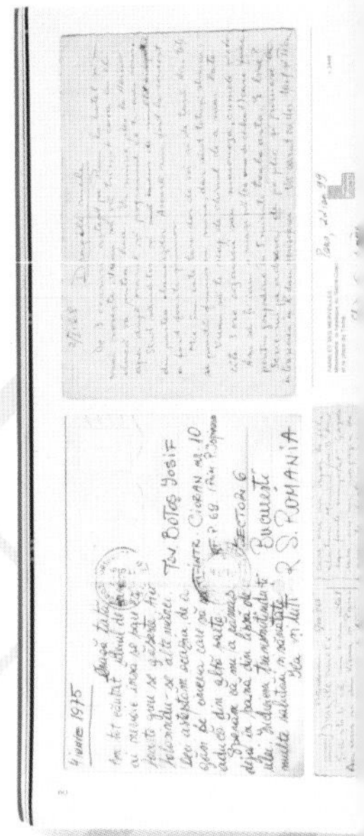

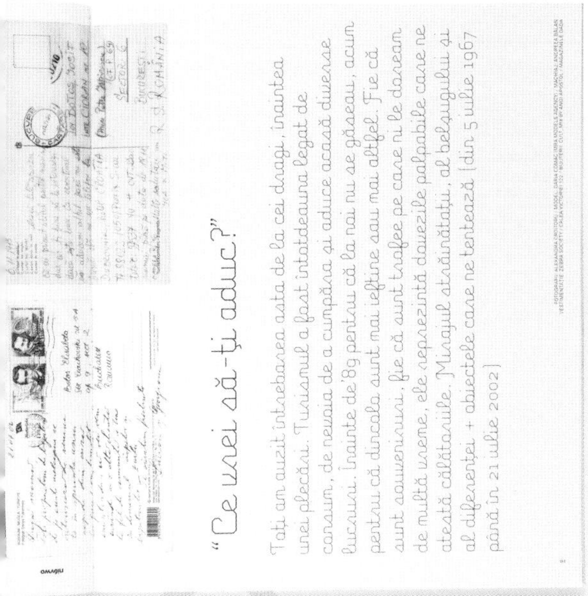
“Ce vrei să-ţi aduc?”
Toţi am auzit întrebarea asta de la cei dragi, înaintea unei plecări. Turismul a fost întotdeauna legat de consum, de nevoia de a cumpăra şi aduce acasă diverse lucruri. Înainte de '89 pentru că la noi nu se găseau, acum pentru că dincolo sunt mai ieftine sau mai altfel. Fie că sunt suveniruri, fie că sunt trofee pe care ni le doream de multă vreme, ele reprezintă dovezile palpabile care ne atestă călătoriile. Mirajul străinătăţii, al belşugului şi al diferenţei + obiectele care ne tentează (din 5 iulie 1967 până în 21 iulie 2002)
OMAGIU

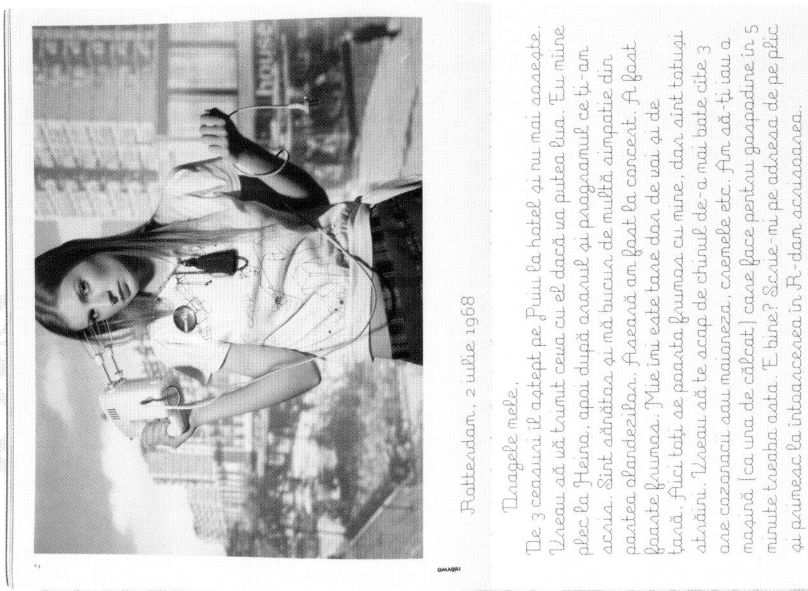
Rotterdam, 2 iulie 1968
Dragele mele,
De 3 ceasuri îl aştept pe Puiu la hotel şi nu mai soseşte. Vreau să vă trimit ceva cu el dacă va putea lua. Eu mâine plec la Heina, apoi după orarul şi programul ce ţi-am scris. Sînt sănătos şi mă bucur de multă simpatie din partea olandezilor. Aseară am fost la concert. A fost foarte frumos. Aici toţi se poartă frumos cu mine, dar sînt totuşi străini. Vreau să te scap de chinul de-a mai bate câte 3 ore cozonacii sau maioneza, cremele etc. Am să-ţi iau o maşină (ca una de călcat) care face pentru gospodine în 5 minute treaba asta. E bine? Scrie-mi pe adresa de pe plic şi primesc la întoarcerea în R-dam scrisoarea.
Vă sărut cu drag.
OMAGIU

SOLOTHURN
BERLIN
SEATTLE
CANNES
UDINE
PRESS PASS
CLERMONT-FERRAND
1999
OMAGIU

CHEAP
&CHIC
360°!
OMAGIU

Art Direction: **Uscha Pohl**
Publisher: **Uscha Pohl/Very Up & Co**
Countries: **USA/UK**

VERY

VERY magazine was started as an extension of Very Up & Co, publisher Uscha Pohl's art and fashion space in Tribeca, New York. The aim of VERY was to bridge the areas of art, fashion, culture, and social issues, and it was one of the first enterprises initiating the "crossover" movement of the fashion/art/design hybrid in the late 1990s.

The editorial content of VERY is a personal selection of projects and reflections, and touches a broad range of subjects, so it is always changing and is never thematic. Pohl collaborates with creatives and artists to develop projects for the magazine. Sometimes contributors lay out their own pages and choose a writer to work with them, and if not, Pohl takes on that role. "The aim is to come as close as possible to the view of the creative or artist," she explains. "Myself and the magazine therefore become a catalyst to their expression. For other occasions I find individuals who work on a particular project, and we find a way to best represent it or their experiences. As we have the spaces in New York and London we are now able to show work three-dimensionally as well as two-dimensionally in the magazine. These are related, but very different exercises on the same subject, which is fascinating."

VERY finds its way through the world and collects like-minded people who care about art and ideas, about individualism and freedom of speech, the present and future. "VERY is meant to inspire and offer an opportunity to publish ideas, thoughts, and projects, which might not necessarily have a chance in more commercial publications, and I think it works," says Pohl. "In our global world we hear fewer and fewer individual voices. I am very happy to be able to contribute mine, however small it might be." The design of the magazine is simple. The idea is to show the projects/artwork as straightforwardly as possible, not unlike hanging an exhibition on a gallery wall.

Today, along with publishing VERY magazine, Pohl also produces the two VERY styleguide series: Fashion, an annual global pocket book for the international fashion/art/design traveler; and the city guides, in which in-the-know people in fashion, music, arts, and acting recommend their favorite spots in their town.

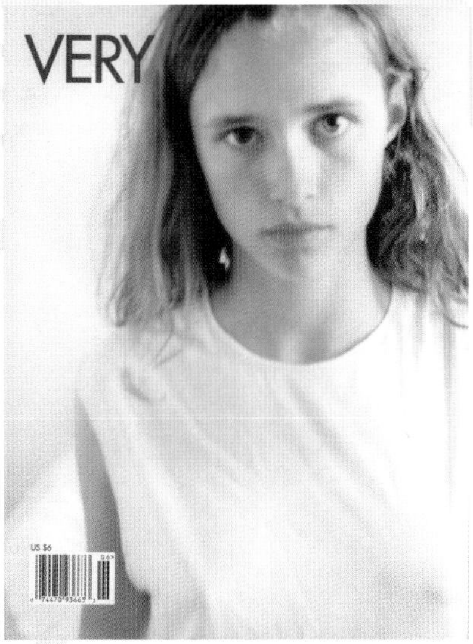

JASON SHULMAN

Harold Edgerton, pioneering high-speed photographer and inventor of the stroboscope, always denied that he was an artist. He simply recorded the moment, that was all. He insisted that the compositions he chose were unfreighted by emotion or symbolism. They were just the best for revealing the dynamics of a splashing milk drop, for example, and that was all.

These pieces by Jason Shulman also deal with unseen landscapes, hyper-speed worlds invisible to us all. Unlike Edgerton's work these are not photographs; they are life-size sculptures.

As I write I'm looking at an ordinary glass tumbler sitting on my desk. Inside it the contrail of bubbles that whizz off a (real) dissolving Solpadeine pill have been paralyzed and solidified in resin at what looks like about a 100,000th of a second. Edgerton's photographic process has been taken and rendered in 3-D.

But, contrary to everything your senses are telling you, this is not a moment of time revealed. This is time sculpted and manipulated. Get a tumbler, fill it with water, and drop a Solpadeine into the liquid. You will see nothing like the controlled and elegant plumes that slide gracefully off Shulman's pills. Instead, the whole glass instantly becomes a crazy mass of seething CO2.

In these pieces, the maniacal effervescing has somehow been tempered and controlled so that you can follow the trail of the pills from the instant they've hit the liquid to their resting place at the bottom of the glass. The Solpadeine sculpture is a fantasy analgesic. It's a dream or an imagining of how these bubbles should / could behave were it not for the earthly reality of hydrodynamics. This is not a real moment in time, it's absolute. Idealised. This is what God takes for his hangover.

C. MARCLAY

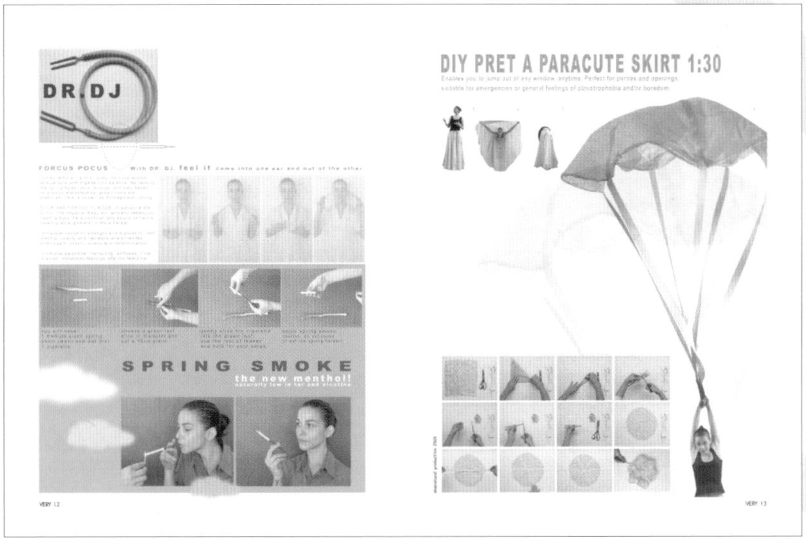

THE PLUNGE

PHOTOGRAPHY: TOMEK SIEREK
STYLING: AGA SIEREK

VERY 22

VERY 23

Body - Pucci

VERY 26

MAKE-UP: LUCY POOK
HAIR: PSHEMKO SIEREK
STARRING: ANNA AND LUCY @ MODELS 1

Pink Bathing Suit - FrontFrench

VERY 27

FADING LIGHT

PHOTOGRAPHY: TOMEK SIEREK, STYLING: AGA SIEREK

VERY 40

Both pages: Jacket Viktor & Rolf, shoes Mark Newson for Nike; fuchsia pants vintage, sunglasses Marechiaro, pink tulle skirt Sierek.

VERY 41

VERY
styleguide
PARIS

VERY
styleguide
RIO DE JANEIRO

VERY
styleguide
NEW YORK

Tom Hingston, Art Director, Stand Off

What is the key to art directing a magazine?
Strength of vision and patience.

Which other magazine would you most like to art direct?
The World of Interiors.

What is the story behind Stand Off?
Stand Off is a biannual magazine published to coincide with the fashion trade show "To Be Confirmed." TBC hosts around 250 independent brands, and the founders were keen to create a magazine which captured the spirit of the event and became a voice for their community.

What inspires the creative idea behind each issue?
Each issue is loosely themed around a chosen city. The main structure of the magazine essentially remains the same from issue to issue. For instance, regular features like the specialist city guide, interviews with brands and designers, or articles about new shops would all be focused on one particular city.

How would you describe Stand Off?
Independent, clever, witty, informative, and beautiful.

Who did you work with to create the magazine and why?
As a design studio, collaboration with photographers and image makers has always formed a fundamental part of our creative approach, and the magazine simply became an extension of this. Photographers, stylists, and illustrators included Angela Moore, Jason Evans, Simon Foxton, Adam Howe, David Hughes, Jeremy Murch, Kam Tang, Izzie Klingels, Mischa Richter, and Gemma Booth.

What is important about the team you work with?
Creating a good magazine combines the skills of great ideas, writing, photography, and design—it is a shared vision. The success of the magazine hinges on that talent working together as one unit, sharing ideas and supporting one another.

How important is the cover image?
The cover is a statement of the magazine's personality. It is the packaging. With the covers for Stand Off we are in a fortunate position because the magazine is distributed free. Without a vending price all the usual constraints that apply to the covers of a newsstand publication are removed. This allows us to be more expressive with the masthead, our choice of cover image, and negates the need for having any straplines or slogans.

Which are your favorite magazine covers of all time and why?
I've always been a huge fan of the Esquire covers George Lois designed in the 1960s. Favorites would have to include his 1968 cover of Muhammad Ali, showing an image of the boxer with arrows stuck in his body, and the 1969 cover of Andy Warhol drowning in a can of tomato soup. They conveyed powerful messages without excess words or straplines. Another all-time favorite is Neville Brody's Face cover featuring "Buffalo Boy" Felix. It's so evocative of its time. In the context of every other title on the newsstand in the early 1980s, it felt really fresh.

What is the future of magazine publishing?
Independent Web sites are the future in magazine publishing. The traffic that can be generated is beginning to far exceed the circulation of even the biggest titles. A great example is a photographer friend's website. The site is just a simple page, updated daily with a new image. He gets around 150,000 hits a month. There just isn't any other publishing platform where his work would receive that level of exposure.

Ralf Herms, Publisher and Art Director, +rosebud

Which are your three favorite magazine covers of all time?
More than single pieces, I find some cover-concepts quite appealing. Many of the TWEN titles from the 1970s, art directed by Willy Fleckhaus. One can still see the quality and revolutionary ideas in typography, photography, and page layout. The Believer covers, arranged within a very straight grid, the typography, the color scheme, and especially the illustrated portraits, make for a unique, but very consistent look. The same goes for Flaunt: the quality of photography and illustration is stunning, combined with brilliant finishing details like die cuts, gatefolds, embossing, and so on.

What is the key to art directing a magazine?
I am working on figuring that out.

Which other magazine would you most like to art direct?
One of the iconic men's magazines like Playboy or Penthouse.

What is the story behind +rosebud magazine?
It started as a graduation project at design university. I tried to come up with a project that actually got in touch with the outside world—nothing virtual or fictional. In 1998 the design-book/magazine market was sparsely populated. Therefore, the combination of naive enthusiasm, fortunate circumstances, and an incredible media response to the premier issue made for a very good start.

What inspires the creative idea behind each issue?
The basic idea of +rosebud is the luxury of constant change. Each issue starts completely from scratch with a new theme, new contributors, new format, new layout, new materials, and new production features.

How would you describe +rosebud?
Lavish content, design, production, and schedules.

How do you approach each issue?
We allow ourselves a lot of time in thinking about the theme for each issue and developing an adequate briefing for potential contributors. During the submission process we curate the presented concepts and finally make a selection of the works that we feel are best for the specific theme. Following that the layout is developed and prepared for production.

Who did you work with to create each issue?
We collaborate with a lot of people from all over the world. Besides "typical" creatives like photographers, illustrators, designers, etc., we also like to get involved with people from other professions: scientists, poets, architects, musicians ... Often we are contacted by people we've never heard of before, which constantly proves to be a very enriching experience.

What is important about the team that you work with?
The commitment to renewal for each and every issue.

How important do you think the cover image on a magazine is?
A good cover corresponds with the rest of the magazine. There is nothing more disappointing than buying a magazine because of its striking cover and finding out that the rest of the content and design cannot keep up with it.

What is the future of magazine publishing?
To me the future of printed media will be decided upon its level of relevance for its readers, especially when the overall design and production quality is constantly improving, the quality of content can make a difference again.

04

"The magazine that looks like an effortless, complete thought usually is the product of a pretty disciplined approach and thorough attention to lots of details."

Colin Metcalf, Art Director, GUM

Navigation

"A good magazine has a balance of visual expression and stimulating articles; it documents expression and emotion."

Ezra Petronio, Art Director, self service

Introduction

Magazine navigation is what gives the designer the opportunity to direct the reader through any given publication. It is also a way of informing the reader of what is in the magazine and what is coming up next as they read through. The contents page or pages, for instance, give the running order of each item featured and also often function as the place for a list of contributors, credits, and contact details. It is therefore essential that the layout and design of this be done in such a way that the information is clear and readable. As shown in this chapter, designers go about this in a variety of ways, making for an interesting selection of very different layouts.

First, divider pages guide the reader through a magazine. They are used to signal the beginning or end of a section or article and are designed in a range of ways: they can take the form of a double-page spread with image and headline or a single image on the left of a double-page spread with the feature beginning on the right-hand page, the list goes on. As well as divider pages, designers often use other methods to indicate section breaks or changes of pace and flow. These can range from changing typeface, to tinting the pages, to the use of different paper stocks, to alternating full-color and black-and-white printing.

The other essential element of a magazine's navigation is the use of headlines and kickers or standfirsts that help the reader determine what they want to read, when they want to read it, and in how much detail. All these elements together are part of traditional magazine-navigation design, and most magazines continue to use them all—however, how designers go about creating them can vary greatly, as is shown in this chapter.

Art Direction: **Nik Dimopoulos/ Timothy Moore**
Publisher: **Shannon Michael Cane**
Country: **Australia**

They Shoot Homos Don't They?

They Shoot Homos Don't They? is described by its publishers as a magazine for men and their admirers. Published in Australia—but with a reader network that spreads across Australia, northern Europe, and the USA—the first issue came out in early 2005.
It aims to provide an alternative reality for the gay and art world. It is glossy, which according to the publishers fools people into a false sense of comfort, but there is a depth to the magazine that rewards those who read between the lines.

Each issue is separated into three sections, titled "Homos," "Shoot," and "They Don't They." The folder page for each combines key images with witty remarks about the content and links everything in the section together in a key visual. "We try to point out basic relations within the content," explains Moore. "We saw the solution being in front of us—as in the content—and we should stop trying too hard to make new meaning. That's why not having an idea made so much sense; we tried not to think too much. We had to deal with the existing condition and collaborate with the contributors to understand their position. As a result, we insert competition or game pages that bridge different contributions."

The "brotherhood" of They Shoot Homos spreads wide. In particular, photographer Jason Evans and artist Scott Redford have been responsive to the "no idea" brief, which relies on process and collaboration rather than delivering an end product for the designers to lay out.

_I'M HAVING THE MOST BEAUTIFUL NIGHTMARE
CRAIG DOTY

IN THIS FOLDER, CONSIDER:
THINKING ABOUT A CLOWN AND PORN
BEARING A TORCH FOR MARIAH CAREY
GETTING A FEEL FOR FANCY PANTS
INDEX:
SCOTT REDFORD 001/008
CHRISTIAN THOMPSON 001/014
EDIE SEDGEWICK 001/020
JASON EVANS 001/026
FOLDER 001/ HOMOS

THEY
SHOOT
HOMOS
DON'T THEY?
002
RRP
AUS $12.50
USA $11.50
EUR €10.00

Art Direction: **Claudia Wu**
Publisher: **Claudia Wu**
Country: **USA**

Me Magazine

First published in fall 2004, each issue of New York-based quarterly Me Magazine explores the life of a guest editor through photographs, interviews, and contributions from their friends. According to Designer and Publisher Claudia Wu, previously of Visionaire and V magazine, the magazine is a reaction to society and today's media values–celebrity, fame, and money—and is about real people reflecting upon where they came from, how they got to where they are now, and their successes and failures.

"I had been working on other people's magazines for years, so when it came to starting my own, I wanted to do something different from the majority of magazines on newsstands today that are either vehicles for selling the newest fashion or products, or showcases for photographers and artists," explains Wu. "Most readers can relate more to people who are still developing themselves and their careers, people who wouldn't be covered in-depth in any other magazine because they haven't accomplished enough yet."

The art direction and design of Me Magazine changes with each issue. Based around the featured guest editor, it is never overpowering, but rather utilitarian and subtle. However, one thing that does stay much the same is the table of contents. For each issue it is designed as a diagram that explains how the guest editor met everyone who is featured. The diagram refers to the dates, people, and events that happened when they met. Always interesting, it is also important for setting that issue of the magazine in context and giving the reader a neat history of the featured guest editor's life or lives.

Benjamin Cho, a friend, & Leo Fitzpatrick

Alex Hawgood & Patrik

Ryan McGinley & Dan Colen

Chris & Tina

Humberto Leon & Michael Bullock

Carolyn, Judith Eisler, Chris, T.Cole, & Lizzi

Me & Hisham

Me#1, meet Me#3

editor's letter

I'm sure we all know someone like Hisham Bharoocha. He's the friend you never see because he's always working on a million projects all at once. Hisham is a musician, photographer, artist, and now the first *Me Magazine* Guest Editor & Photographer. It was a daunting feat that he somehow accomplished while working on photography assignments for other people, travelling to L.A. and Hawaii, turning twenty-nine, playing numerous shows as his new one-man band Soft Circle, creating art for group shows, and stopping by the launch of *Me*#3. We were pleased to see him taking a break and mingling with past, present, and possible future *Me* contributors at Sway last March. Djs Brian DeGraw and Suzanne Ackerman kept everyone entertained, and at midnight everyone wished Anna Steiner a happy birthday while her favorite Smiths song played over the sound system. Thanks to Lynda Garcia, the staff at Sway, Makiko Okada, and Michael Bullock for all their help in making the event possible.

—Claudia Wu

all photos by Eleanor Chung

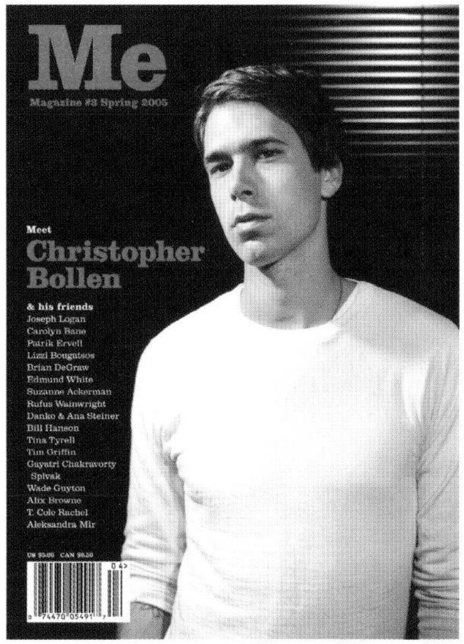
Me
Magazine #3 Spring 2005
Meet
Christopher Bollen
& his friends
Joseph Logan
Carolyn Bane
Patrik Ervell
Lizzi Bougatsos
Brian DeGraw
Edmund White
Suzanne Ackerman
Rufus Wainwright
Danko & Ana Steiner
Bill Hanson
Tina Tyrell
Tim Griffin
Gayatri Chakravorty Spivak
Wade Guyton
Alix Browne
T. Cole Rachel
Aleksandra Mir
US $5.00 CAN $6.50

me
Magazine #4 Summer 2005
hisham bharoocha
4

Me
Magazine #2 Winter 2004
Meet
Miho
Aoki
and her friends
Rusty Santos
Justine D.
Sidney Prawatyotin
Vito Acconci
Mira Billotte
assume vivid astro focus
Ju Kim
Susan Cianciolo
Benjamin Liu
Rosalie Knox
Dave Portner
Tracy Nakayama
John Minh Nguyen
Ion Birch

Me
MAGAZINE #5 AUTUMN 2005
Rivington Arms
Mirabelle Marden
& Melissa Bent
with
Darren Bader
Mathew Cerletty
Daniel Colen
Philippa Craze
Max Farago
John Finneran
Jaclyn Hodes
Leigh Johnson
Hanna Liden
Melia Marden
Annabel Mehran
Peter Miles
Sahra Motalebi
Carter Mull
Benedicte Sebested
Dash Snow
Pinar Yolacan
Margarite Wade
US $5.00 CAN $6.50

Me
Habitual

Art Direction: **Andrew Clare**
Publisher: **Plan B Publishing Ltd**
Country: **UK**

Plan B

Plan B was launched in 2004. It builds on the success of Editor-in-Chief Everett True's acclaimed previous magazine Careless Talk Costs Lives, extending its remit to cover counterculture in literature, movies, comics, video games, visual arts, and music. It has established itself as a strong title both for its written content and the high quality of photography and illustration that is a feature throughout.

Art Director Andrew Clare doesn't have set design rules as such. "I try and give the artists as much freedom as possible, and work with what I get," he explains, but, despite this, there is a consistency to the look of each issue of Plan B. An interesting feature is the use of handwritten headlines for articles, so giving every feature its own distinct personality. Clare works with a broad range of photographers and illustrators for each issue, which makes for a visually stimulating read.

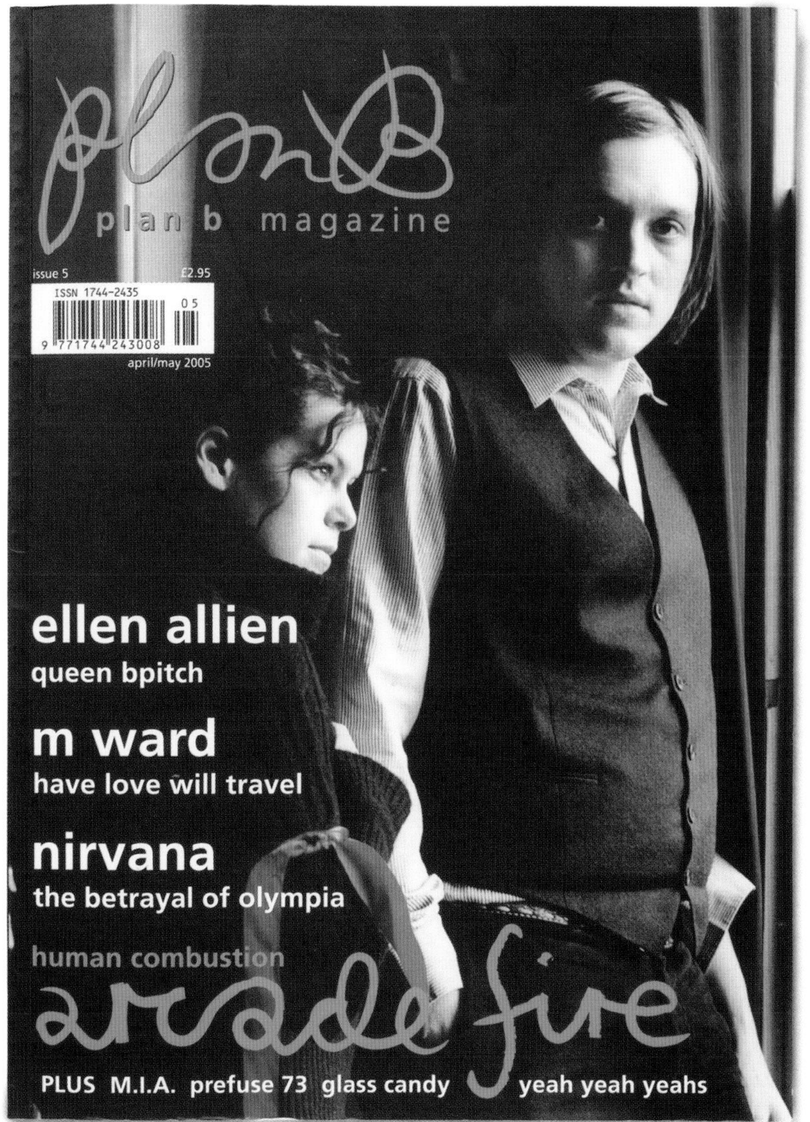

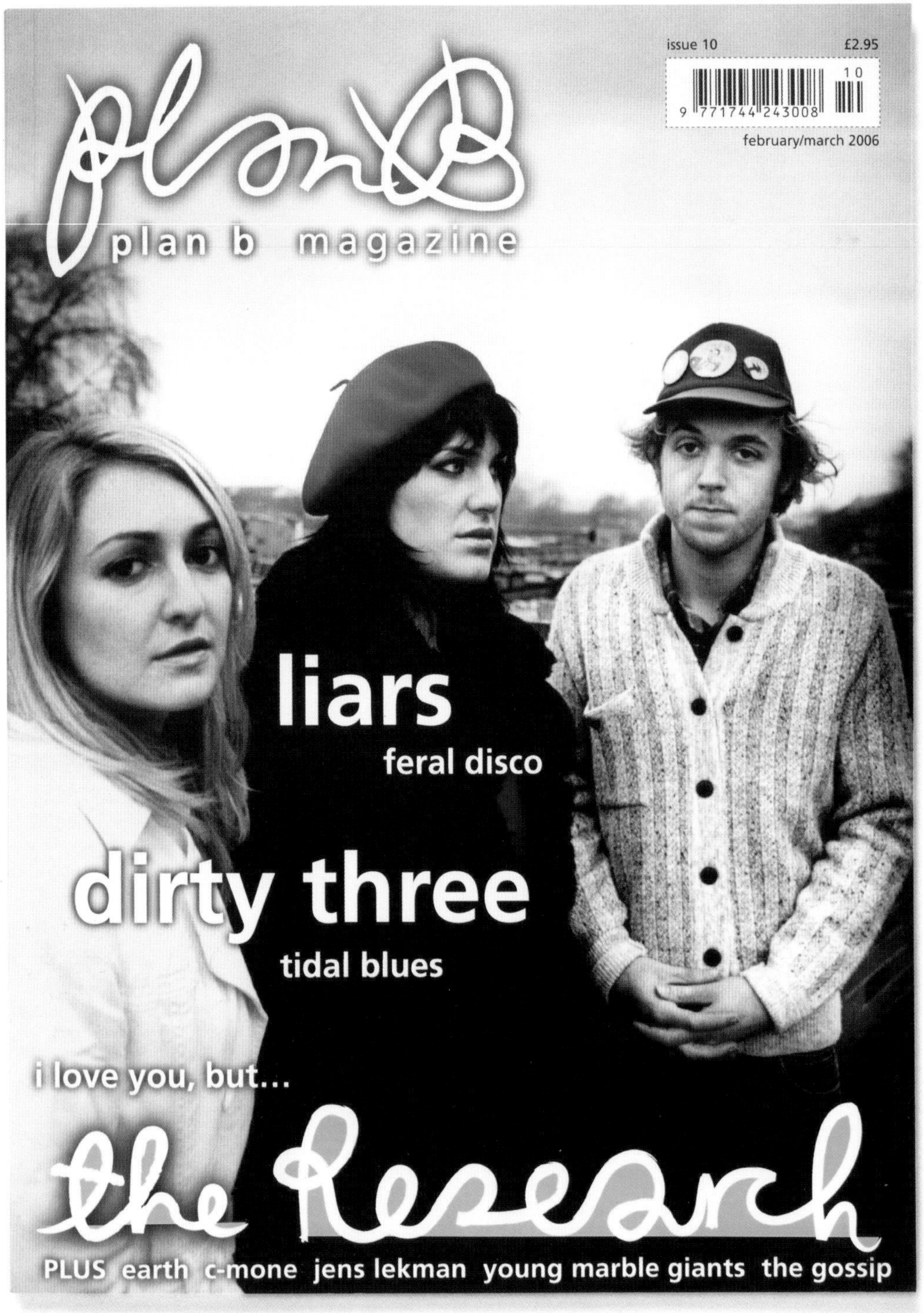
issue 10
£2.95
february/march 2006
plan b
plan b magazine
liars
feral disco
dirty three
tidal blues
i love you, but...
the Research
PLUS earth c-mone jens lekman young marble giants the gossip

yeah yeah yeahs

the void
Fashion
true colours
The Pamflet guide to joining the rainbow revolution
Take inspiration from Cyndi Lauper, MIA and Kate 'Fancy Socks' Long Blondes

Queen
bpitch
Submitting to the sound of Ellen Allien's future metal beats
'To turn myself inside out while I make music is one of my favourite hobbies'

i love you, but...
Love, trust, betrayal. Keyboards, drums, harmonies. Russell, Sarah, Georgia
Miss AMP meets The Research

BURN TO SHINE: WASHINGTON DC 01.14.2004
WILLIAM ELLIOTT WHITMORE
FINGERS CUT MEGAMACHINE
10 YEARS AND STILL COOL AS FUCK

Art Direction: **Tom Hingston Studio**
Publisher: **Brand Progression and VICE**
Country: **UK**

Stand Off

Shown here is the pilot issue of Stand Off, published in July 2004 and designed by Tom Hingston, Manuela Wyss, and Simon Gofton at Tom Hingston Studio. The founders were keen to create a magazine that captured the spirit of fashion shows and became a voice for their community of fashion creatives, marketers, and managers. Edited by Alex Ashcroft, designed and art directed by Tom Hingston Studio, and copublished by Brand Progression and VICE, the magazine is mainly sent out to creatives, though a large number are bound with VICE magazine and distributed at fashion shows and associated parties, events, and exhibitions.

There are two sections to the publication: The Magazine and The Guide. The Magazine aims to be an informative and entertaining, must-have title for the fashion community, including features, interviews, and so on. The Guide is a comprehensive listing of all the brands showing at the relevant shows, with contact details for each. Designwise, each issue is loosely themed around a different chosen city and the main structure of the magazine remains the same from issue to issue. There are regular features, such as the chosen city guide, interviews with brands and designers, and articles about new shops in that city.

Tom Hingston Studio works with many creatives to create each issue. "As a design studio, collaboration with photographers and image-makers has always formed a fundamental part of our creative approach. The magazine simply became an extension of this," explains Hingston. Photographers, stylists, and illustrators include Angela Moore, Jason Evans, Simon Foxton, Jeremy Murch, and Kam Tang. The cover photography for this issue was by Angela Moore.

A meeting with
Norman Jay
At 46, DJ supreme,
MBE and the man
behind the Good
Times Sound System
busting tunes at the
forthcoming 40th
anniversary of the
Notting Hill Carnival,
Norman Jay is the
daddy of old school.
Stand Off checks
what's hidden in the
spinmaster's wardrobe

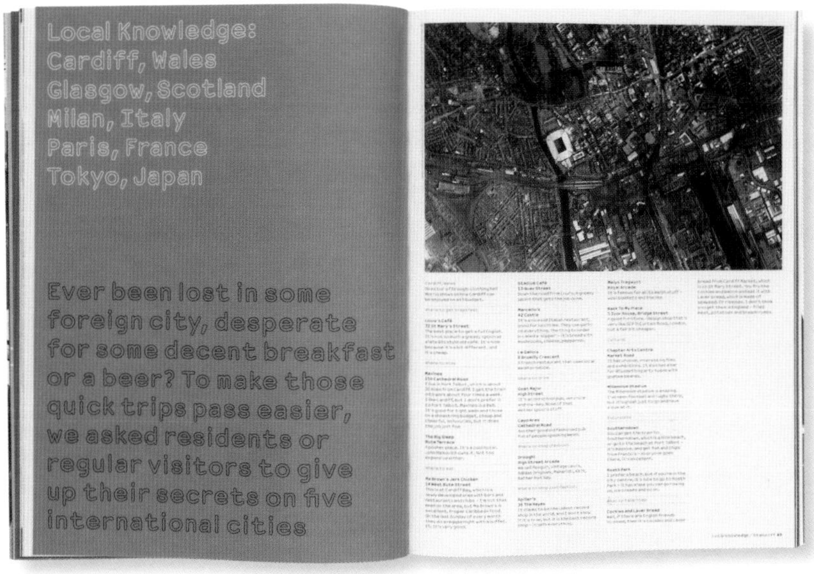
Local Knowledge:
Cardiff, Wales
Glasgow, Scotland
Milan, Italy
Paris, France
Tokyo, Japan
Ever been lost in some foreign city, desperate for some decent breakfast or a beer? To make those quick trips pass easier, we asked residents or regular visitors to give up their secrets on five international cities

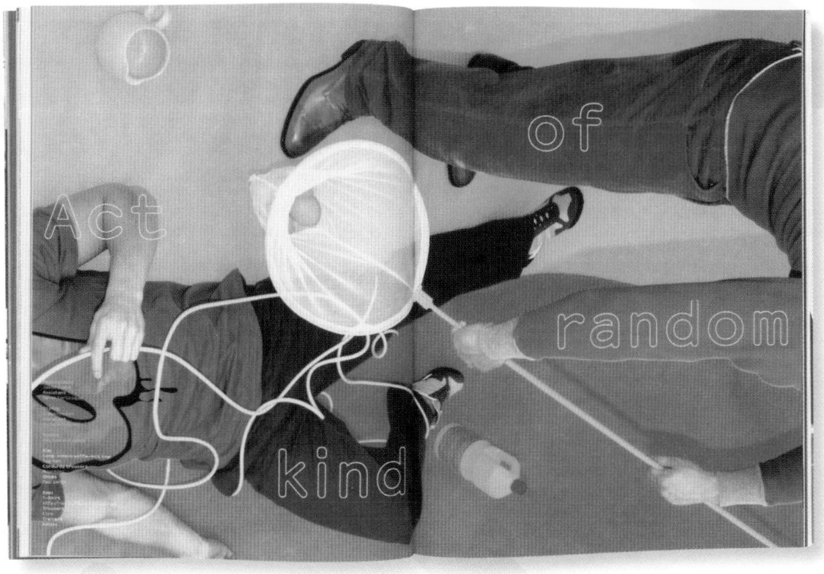
Act
of
random
kind

Acid

Art Direction: **Made Thought**
Publisher: **Grafik**
Country: **UK**

Grafik.

Grafik—formerly Graphics International—aims to showcase current trends and approaches to graphic design around the world, and it features the best of both cutting-edge and commercial work, so providing a platform for photography, art, typography, illustration, new media, fashion, technology, and advertising.

First published in 1984, the readership now stretches throughout the USA, Europe, Asia, and Australia. In 2003 London-based designers MadeThought were approached by the editor and asked to "design a magazine that encapsulated the spirit and expression of the work it was showcasing." The result was a radically different magazine, with a name change, a new format, and a change in vocabulary as well as image style.

"Our aim was to create a magazine that reacted to the specific content of each article and that followed no fixed template," explains designer Ben Parker. "This afforded us flexibility in the design so it could be appropriate to the content we were laying out. This, in turn, allowed us the freedom to develop and push the vocabulary of the magazine."

The redesign proved a success, with a 30 percent increase in readership during the first year. The contents of each issue are displayed on the cover, and each page and spread is visually pleasing and easy to read without being predictable.

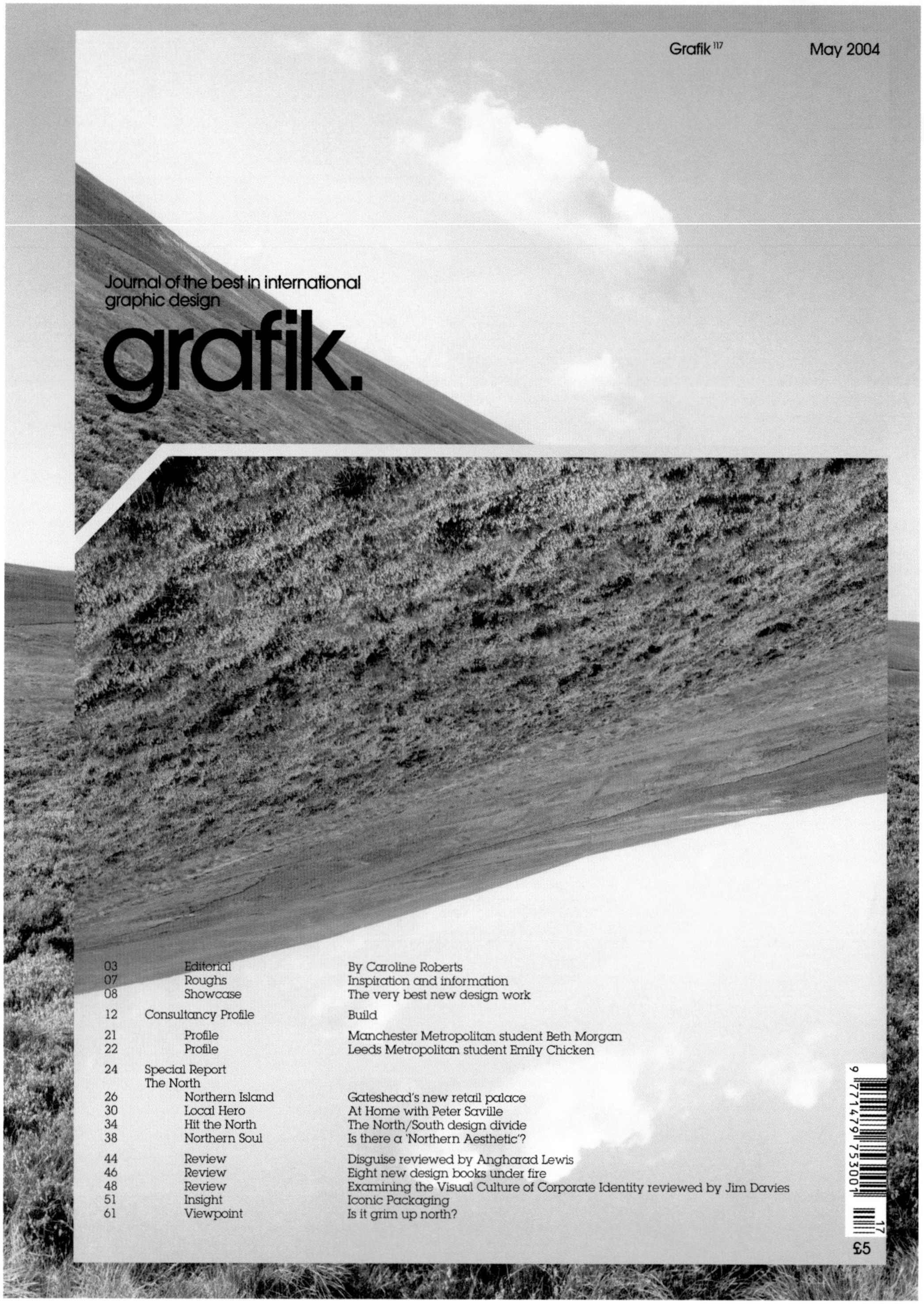

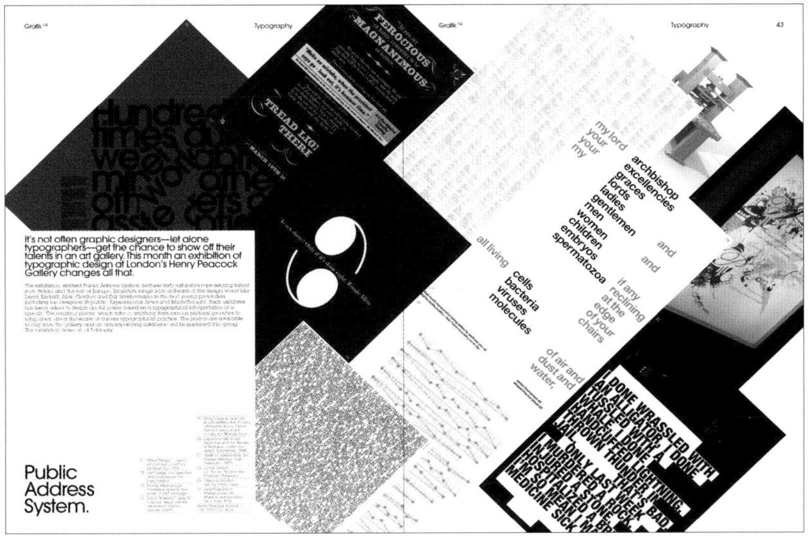
Grafik
Typography
43
It's not often graphic designers—let alone typographers—get the chance to show off their talents in an art gallery. This month an exhibition of typographic design at London's Henry Peacock Gallery changes all that.
Public Address System.
FEROCIOUS
MAGNANIMOUS
my lord
your
your
my
archbishop
excellencies
graces
lords
ladies
gentlemen
men
women
children
embryos
spermatozoa
and
and
all living
cells
bacteria
viruses
molecules
if any
reclining
at the
edge
of your
chairs
of air and
dust and
water,

Grafik
Special Report
Seduction
28
29
Special Report
Seduction
Hot Pants.
Aural Sex.
Seduce and Awe.
Brazen Images.
Forbidden
Fruit.

Grafik
Special Report
2003—How was it for you?
37
Helvetica
Serif
CHIRAC
KAN IKKE
DAGEN
Matthew Carter:
Big Caslon Italic,
Wallpaper.
Mark Errington:
Helvetica Serif.
James Goggin:
Olafur Eliasson's
Weather Project,
Tate Modern.
Unknown:
Ornamented wood
type alphabet.
Jeremy Tankard:
Aspect.
Jeremy Johnson:
Formé.
Emma Eldridge
Identify+Devise.
Jonas Heckscher:
Dagen.
Natascha French:
Read.
Dalton Maag:
Tesco Astound.

Special Report
The North
24
Grafik
Special Report
The North
25
Special Report
The North
Northern Island. 26
Local Hero. 30
Hit the North.
34
Northern Soul. 38
Is It Grim
Up North?

Grafik
32
Profiles
33
Christopher Lane.
grafik for £45

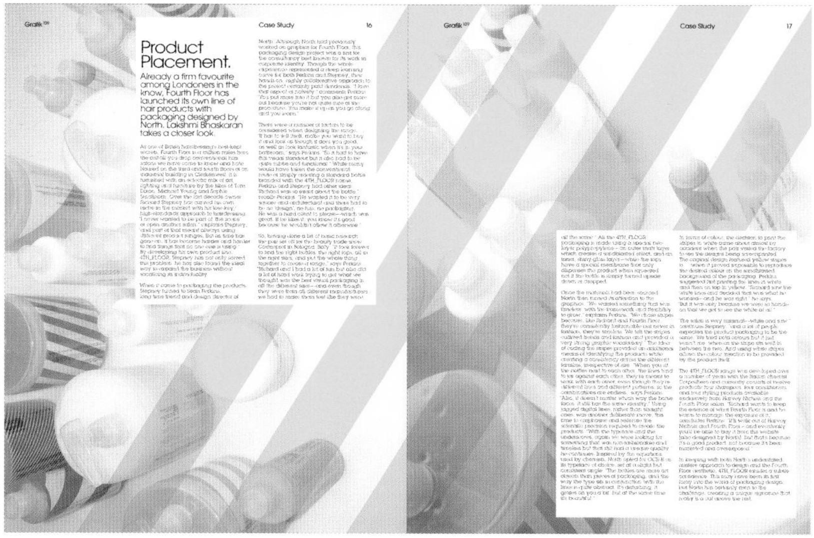
Grafik
Case Study
16
Product Placement.
Already a firm favourite among Londoners in the know, Fourth Floor has launched its own line of hair products with packaging designed by North. Lakshmi Bhaskaran takes a closer look.
Grafik
Case Study
17

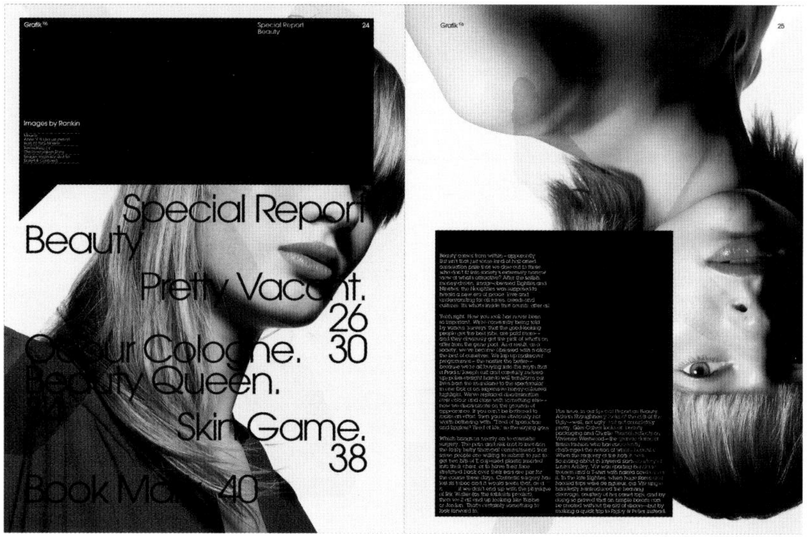
Grafik
Special Report Beauty
24
Grafik
25
Images by Rankin
Special Report
Beauty
Pretty Vacant.
26
Odour Cologne.
30
Beauty Queen.
Skin Game.
38
Book Mark.
40

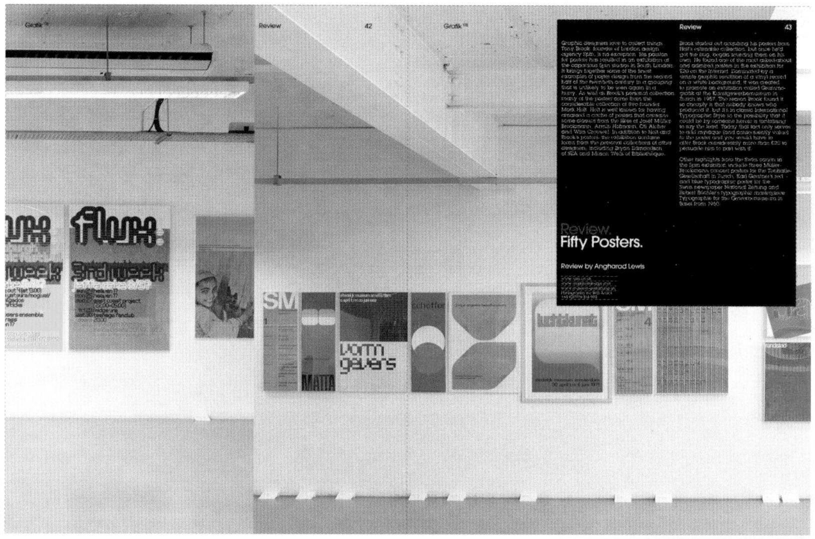
Grafik
Review
42
Grafik
Review
43
Review.
Fifty Posters.
Review by Angharad Lewis

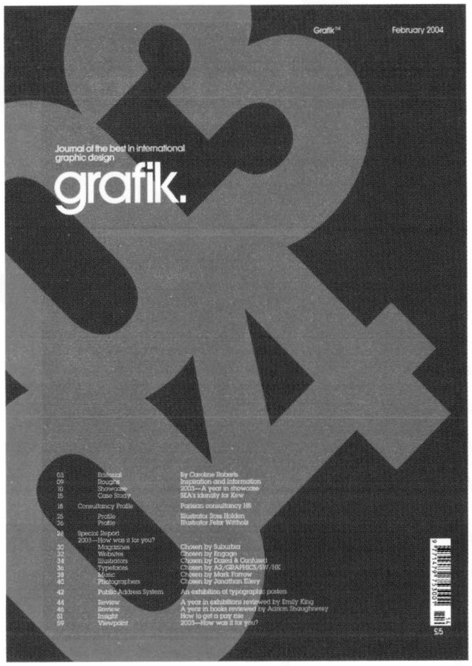
Grafik114
February 2004
Journal of the best in international graphic design
grafik.
03 Editorial By Caroline Roberts
09 Roughs Inspiration and information
10 Showcase 2003—A year in showcase
15 Case Study SEA's identity for Kew
18 Consultancy Profile Parisian consultancy H5
28 Special Report 2003—How was it for you?
30 Magazines Chosen by Suburbia
32 Websites Chosen by Engage
34 Illustrators Chosen by Dazed & Confused
36 Typefaces Chosen by A2/GRAPHICS/SW/HK
38 Music Chosen by Mark Farrow
40 Photographers Chosen by Jonathan Ellery
42 Public Address System An exhibition of typographic posters
44 Review A year in exhibitions reviewed by Emily King
51 Insight How to get a pay rise
59 Viewpoint 2003—How was it for you?
£5

January 2004
Special Report
Journal of the best in international graphic design
grafik.
Special
Report
Experi-
mentation
03 Editorial By Caroline Roberts
09 Roughs Inspiration and information
10 Showcase The very best new design work
14 Consultancy Profile Non-Format
26 Experimentalism New ways of working
34 Come Together Four design collectives reveal all
44 Case Study The first-ever YCN annual
53 Insight The Collection 2003
61 Viewpoint How can commercial work be experimental?
£5

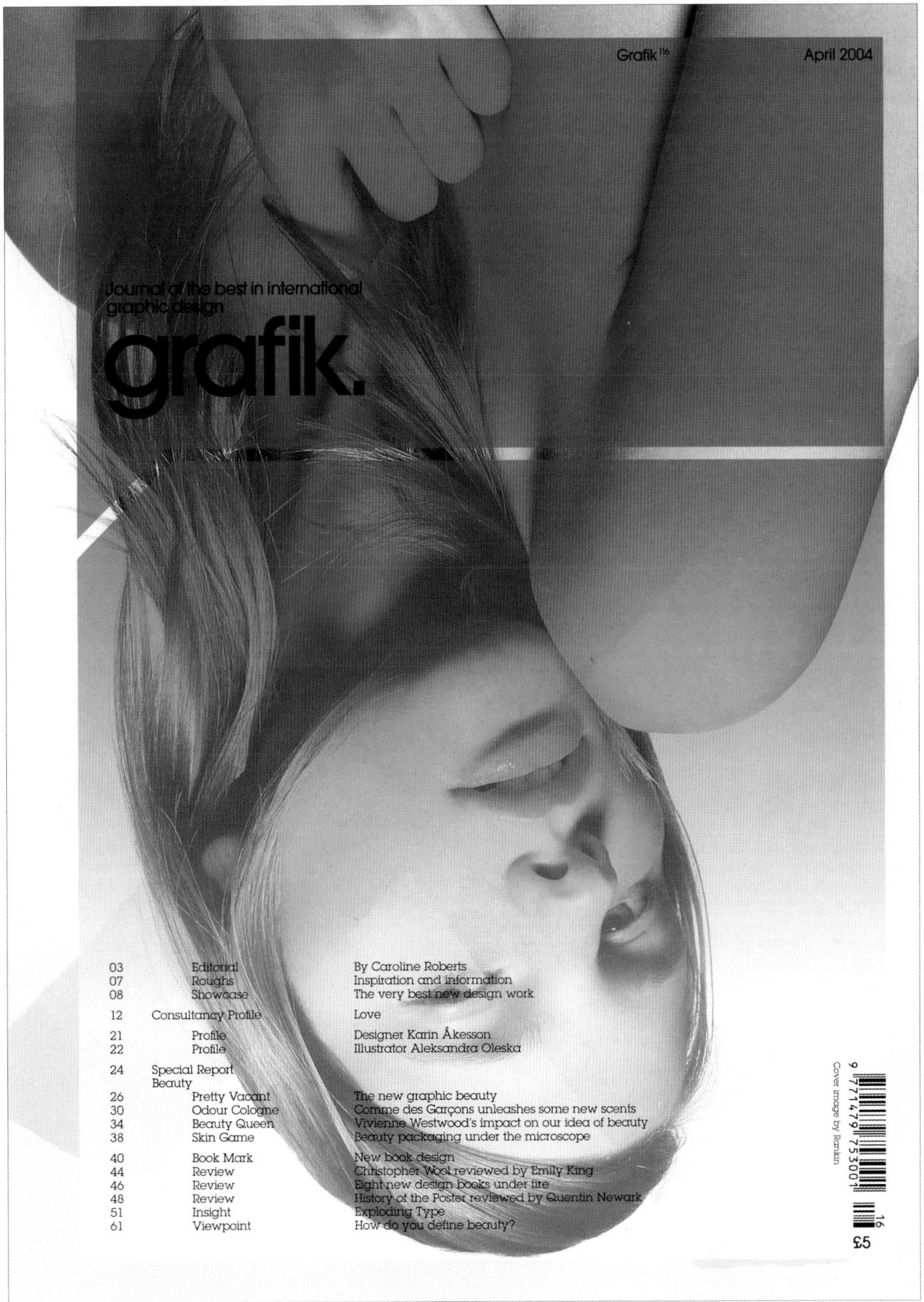
Grafik116
April 2004
Journal of the best in international graphic design
grafik.
03 Editorial By Caroline Roberts
07 Roughs Inspiration and information
08 Showcase The very best new design work
12 Consultancy Profile Love
21 Profile Designer Karin Åkesson
22 Profile Illustrator Aleksandra Oleska
24 Special Report Beauty
26 Pretty Vacant The new graphic beauty
30 Odour Cologne Comme des Garçons unleashes some new scents
34 Beauty Queen Vivienne Westwood's impact on our idea of beauty
38 Skin Game Beauty packaging under the microscope
40 Book Mark New book design
44 Review Christopher Wool reviewed by Emily King
46 Review Eight new design books under fire
48 Review History of the Poster reviewed by Quentin Newark
51 Insight Exploding Type
61 Viewpoint How do you define beauty?
Cover image by Rankin
£5

Art Direction: **Kjell Ekhorn/Jon Forss at Non-Format**
Publisher: **The Wire Magazine Ltd.**
Country: **UK**

Wire

Wire is a UK-based, independent, music monthly magazine that aims to offer in-depth insights into all strands of contemporary music from the past, present, and future—as the masthead reads: "Adventures in Modern Music." It was founded in 1982 by Anthony Wood, and has since undergone many design changes. Shown here is that of designers Kjell Ekhorn and Jon Forss at Non-Format, which first appeared in April 2001.

Wire is primarily a readers' magazine—features often contain between 2,000 and 4,000 words—and Ekhorn and Forss's challenge was to make this large amount of text look accessible by balancing it against the use of good photography. They also wanted to reflect the contemporary nature of the content in the design. "We stripped back the magazine's structure to its bare bones and implemented a Modernist grid that owes a great debt to designers such as Josef Müller-Brockman," explains Forss. "We chose a typeface for the body text that would allow for a great many words to fit on a page, but not look too compact, and we tried, where possible, to allow room for full-page photographs."

The body text used is Franklin Gothic and the cover and sub-heading typography is Akzidenz Grotesk. The headline typefaces change often, sometimes from one issue to the next.

Inside

Afrirampo 10
My Cat Is An Alien 12
Nils Økland 14
Dälek 16
Invisible Jukebox 20
Glenn Jones
Joanna Newsom 24
Zeitkratzer 26
LCD Soundsystem 32
2004 Rewind 38

Regulars
The Masthead 4
Letters 6
Bitstream 8
Global Ear 18
Charts 50
Out There 94
Subscribe 98
Back Issues 100
Epiphanies 106

Reviews
Index 51
Soundcheck 52
Print Run 78
Cross Platform 80
On Location 84

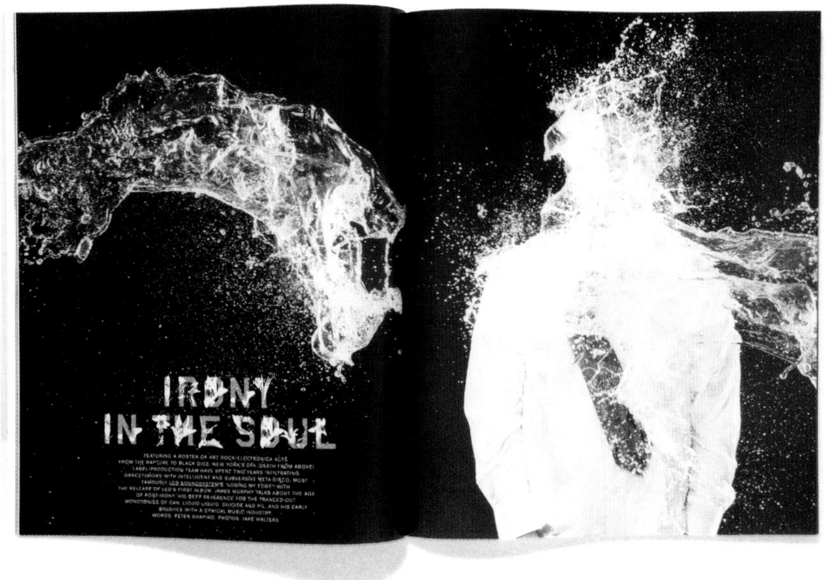

Mike Patton
Fantômas hysteria
Ira Cohen
Elliott Sharp Grime Richard Barrett Venetian Snares MIA

Repeat after me
In Praise of the Riff
Marshall Allen
The Finnish underground
John Peel RIP
Greg Davis
irr. app. (ext.)

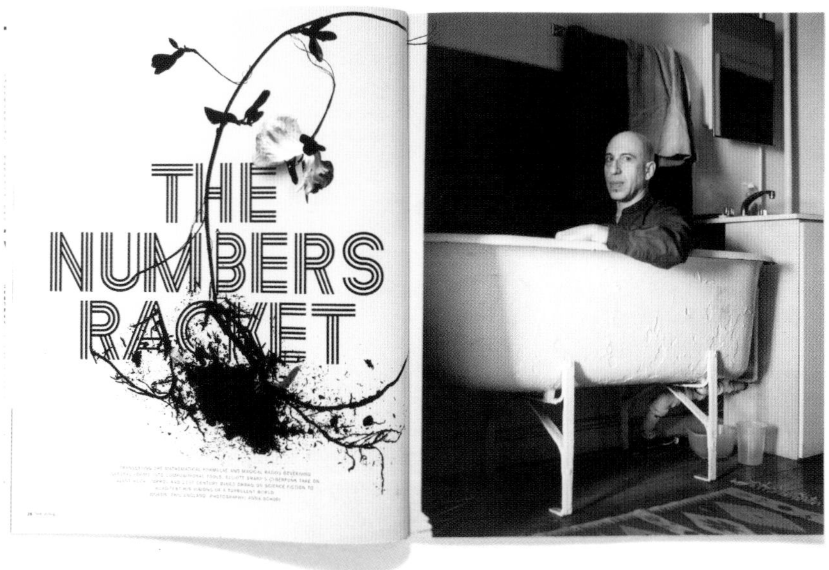
THE NUMBERS RACKET

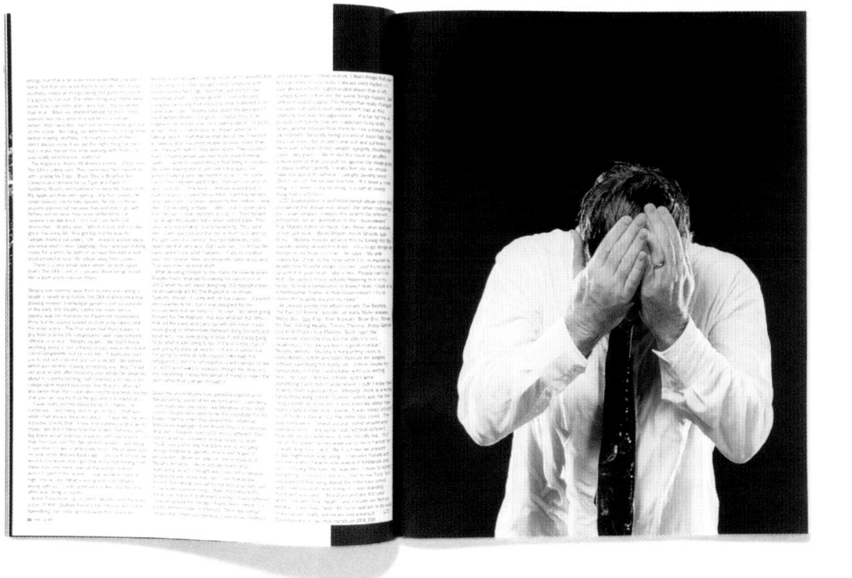

Art Direction: **Sally A. Edwards**
Publishers: **Sally A. Edwards/Sarah J. Edwards**
Country: **UK**

Blag

Established as a fanzine in 1992, a magazine in 1995, a book in 1999, a Web site in 2000, and a magazine—as it is today—in 2004, Blag is about music, movies, fashion, and art. It is a down-to-earth, friendly, edgy, humorous publication started by twin sisters Sally and Sarah Edwards while they were studying graphic design and fashion design, respectively, at art college.

"We started it for various reasons: to get some excitement in our lives, so I could do more graphics and Sarah could do more photography, and because we both loved magazines," explains Sally.

After a break, Blag was relaunched in 2004. The design is classic and refreshingly simple, allowing the content room to breathe. "I'd say the overall Blag style is inspired by classic film work by Saul Bass and Hitchcock, as well as contemporaries, including Wes Anderson and Mike Mills," explains Sally. "We can get inspired by the narrative of a film for the style of a story and that can continue into Sarah's photography and my design. I think there is a secret recipe to our thinking and how we translate one art form as an inspiration for another."

Each issue opens with a simple yet bold double-page spread featuring a message—for instance "Please Enjoy" or "Try Me"—which is designed to set the tone of the issue. The design esthetic is carried through to the opening spreads of features, as shown here. Photography is mainly by Sarah, but the sisters have collaborated with other photographers including Jermaine Francis and Andrew Woffinden.

COMMON

IMPROVISE
PLEASE
ENJOY

TRY
ME*

blag
BLAG
blag
VOL. 2 NØ 3 SUMMER 2005
VOL 2 NØ 3 £4.95
SUMMER 2005
ISSN 1366-4522

Art Direction: **Mark Constantine**
Publisher: **Enter**
Country: **UK**

Exit

Exit magazine is aimed at "high-living, leisure-loving culture addicts, style innovators, and opinion formers" passionate about art, fashion, and photography. It showcases a range of talent from around the world, and contributors have included Wim Wenders, William Eggleston, Inez van Lamsweerde, Miles Aldridge, Amanda de Cadenet, Jamie Hewlett, Tracey Emin, and Takashi Murakami.

The magazine opens with short fashion, beauty, and art articles before leading into the work of the featured contributors. Each one has between four and eight spreads in which to showcase their work, which is simply laid out with plenty of clean white space, and the large format of the magazine makes it more like looking through an art book. Akzidenz Grotesk and Caslon typefaces are used throughout, but a new headline face is introduced in each issue. Colorwise the covers change from issue to issue, but always retain the two-color mix of background and text.

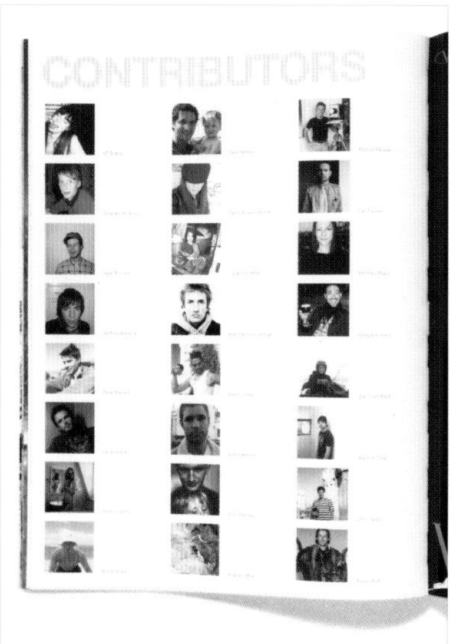

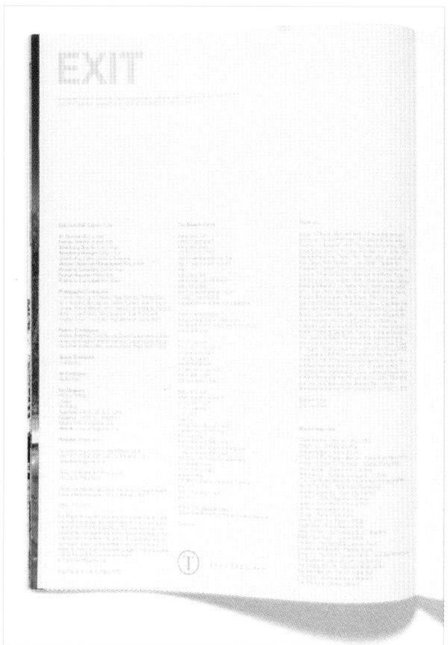

Lisa
Sara
Ola
Rachel
Christelle
Vanessa
Morgan
Valerie
Adina
Photography Randall Mesdon
Fashion Alastair Mackimm

Gegenlicht
Photography Alessandro Dal Buoni

La Belle

Creative Direction: **Vince Frost**
Design: **Vince Frost/Matt Willey/Anthony Donovan/Tim Murphy**
Publisher: **Simon Finch**
Country: **UK**

Zembla/Little Z

Launched in September 2003, Zembla is an international literary magazine. Published five times a year, Zembla combines literary culture with the innovation and flair of a style magazine. The concept was based on the need for a cool literary magazine that targeted a younger audience, but would also attract high-end advertisers such as Paul Smith and Gucci.

Editor, Dan Crowe, and Publisher, Simon Finch, approached Vince Frost and his team at Frost Design to design and art direct it. The brief was short: "Do whatever you want. Be expressive. Have fun with words." The confidence of Zembla's design lies largely in its refusal to adhere to the traditional rules of magazine design. The letter "Z," which spans the entire front cover, forms the masthead and identity of the magazine, while flexible type sizes and characters and a grid that appears "only when we need it" characterize the design within.

Zembla is very much about ideas-based design, and its slogan "Fun with Words" applies equally to both content and form. Arete Mono and Palatino typefaces have been used throughout, giving Zembla its unique look and feel. Little Z—shown on page 115—is aimed at children, and was attached as a special to Zembla Issue 8.

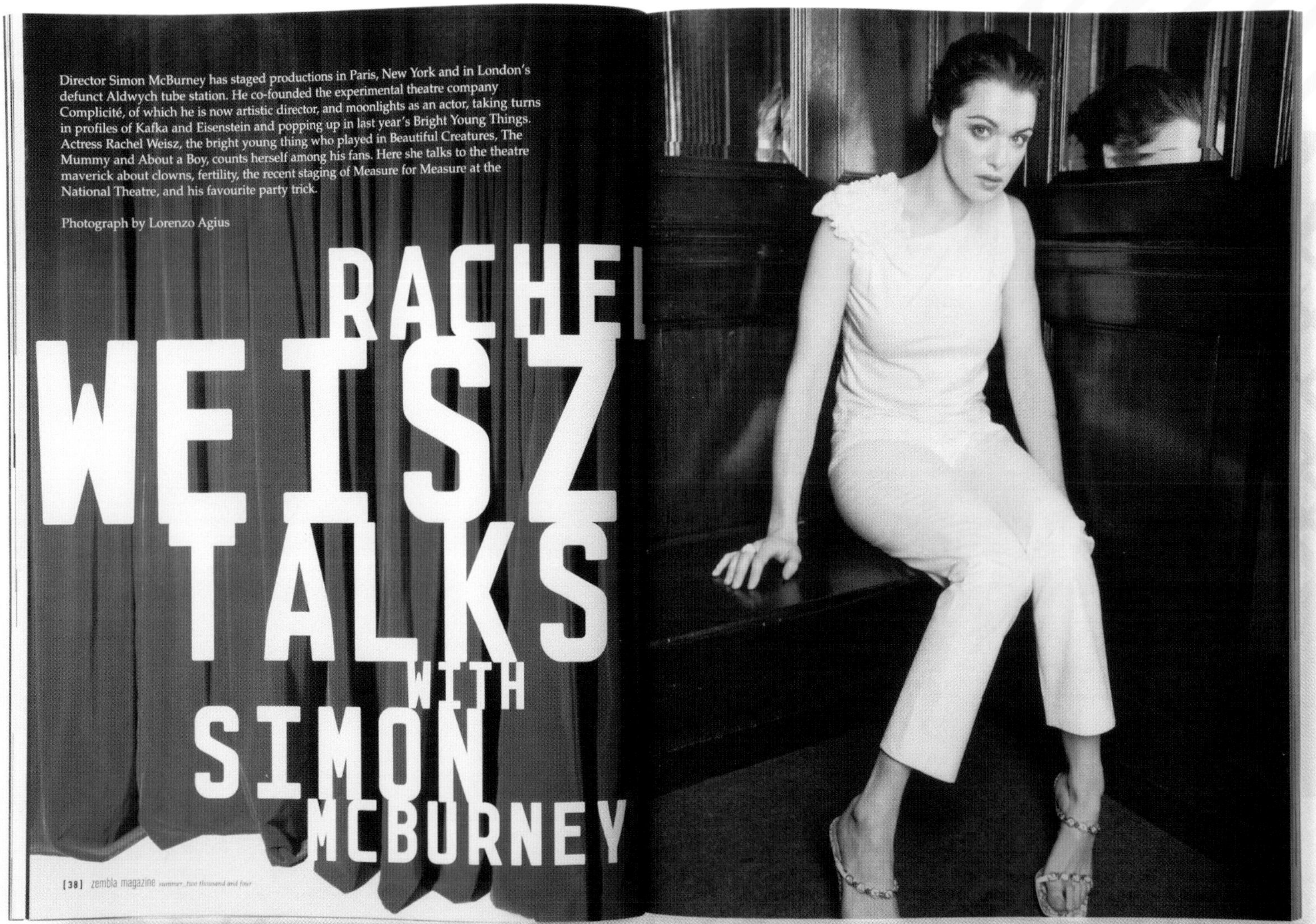

Director Simon McBurney has staged productions in Paris, New York and in London's defunct Aldwych tube station. He co-founded the experimental theatre company Complicité, of which he is now artistic director, and moonlights as an actor, taking turns in profiles of Kafka and Eisenstein and popping up in last year's Bright Young Things. Actress Rachel Weisz, the bright young thing who played in Beautiful Creatures, The Mummy and About a Boy, counts herself among his fans. Here she talks to the theatre maverick about clowns, fertility, the recent staging of Measure for Measure at the National Theatre, and his favourite party trick.

Photograph by Lorenzo Agius

RACHEL WEISZ TALKS WITH SIMON MCBURNEY

[38] zembla magazine summer_two thousand and four

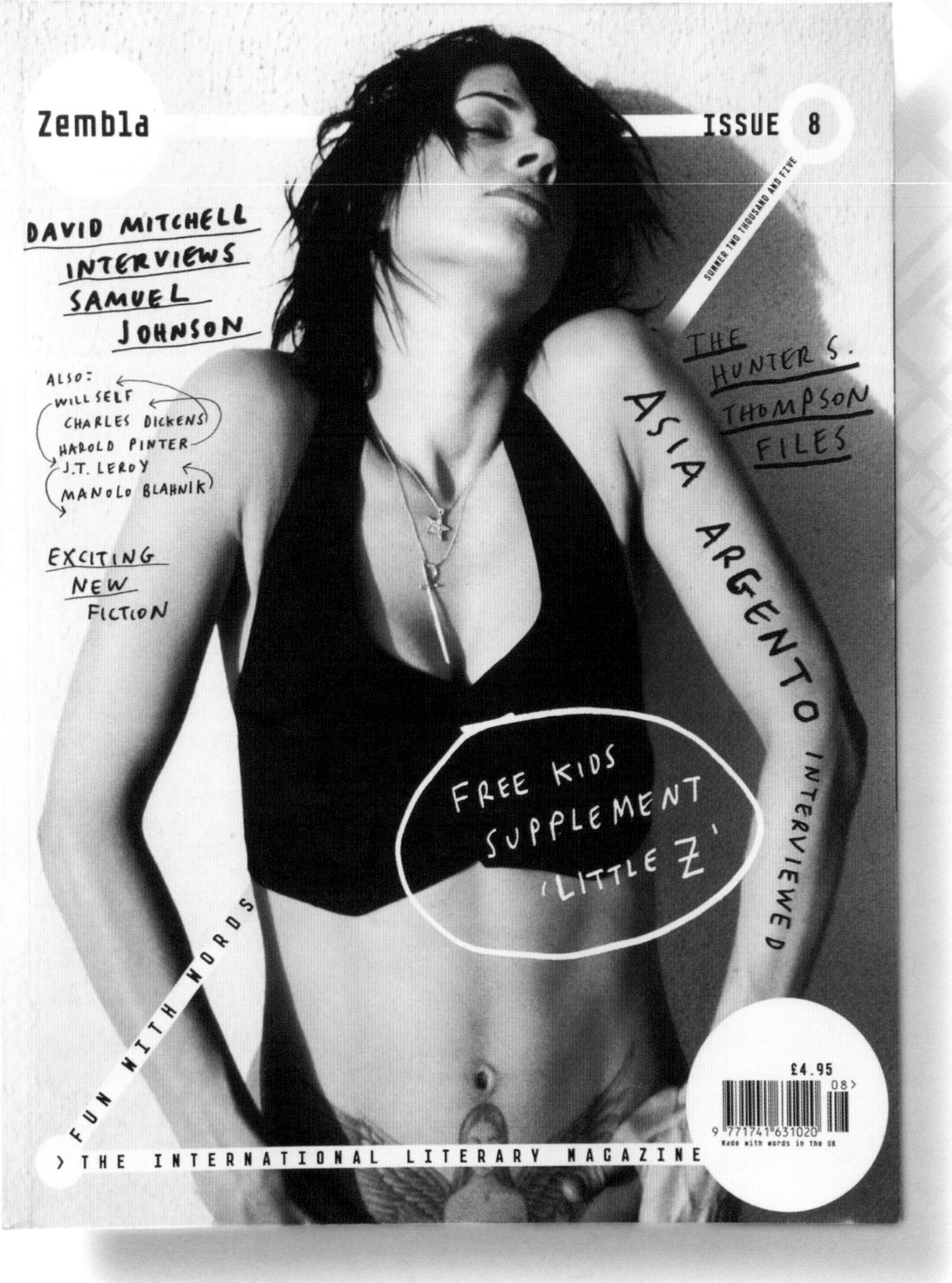
Zembla
ISSUE 8
SUMMER TWO THOUSAND AND FIVE
DAVID MITCHELL INTERVIEWS SAMUEL JOHNSON
ALSO:
WILL SELF
CHARLES DICKENS
HAROLD PINTER
J.T. LEROY
MANOLO BLAHNIK
EXCITING NEW FICTION
THE HUNTER S. THOMPSON FILES
ASIA ARGENTO INTERVIEWED
FREE KIDS SUPPLEMENT 'LITTLE Z'
FUN WITH WORDS
THE INTERNATIONAL LITERARY MAGAZINE
£4.95
08
Made with words in the UK

THE DOGS

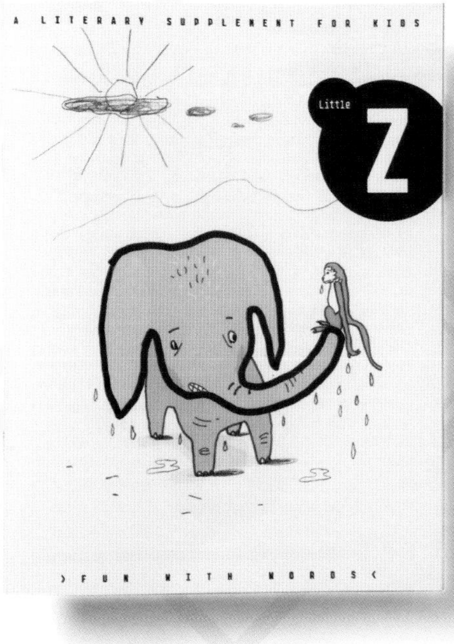
A LITERARY SUPPLEMENT FOR KIDS
Little
Z
>FUN WITH WORDS<

14
the menidakis affair
_There's something strange in the bedroom.
But mind your step. Get stuck into this scary story by Joe Craig.

8
donald and benoît
and the Dancing Devildogs of Fishertown

FANTASTIC FOODS THAT CHANGED THE WORLD
4
The Story of the potato
THE MIGHTY SPUD
MASH
CHIPS
CRISPS
JACKET
ROAST

Art Direction: **Markus Dreßen**
Publisher: **Spectormag GbR/Markus Dreßen/Anne König/Jan Wenzel**
Country: **Germany**

spector cut+paste

spector cut+paste was founded by its three publishers, Markus Dreßen, Anne König, and Jan Wenzel, in 2000. Its aim is to address issues in all cultural areas in a way that truly integrates critical writing with graphic design, something its founders felt couldn't be found in most other comparable magazines. "We wanted to publish a magazine that would allow dialogue and cooperation between different spheres of modern art, and in which the similarities between contents in individual fields would become apparent," explains König.

From the beginning they wanted their design to establish a perfectly developed relationship between image, text, and graphic design. "We are not just talking here about the image illustrating the text or the design giving a more attractive appearance to the magazine," continues König. "What it is really all about is creating a debate between contents in these three fields."

For each issue the graphic designer is involved from the very early stages, becoming part of the editorial process, including selection and commissioning. This has resulted in some interesting and unusual ideas. The second issue, for example, was concerned with fiction and documentation, and was produced in the guise of a laptop in order to reflect this. "We felt the prevalence of the computer today blurs the line between reality and virtual life. The card cover is blank, but for a repetitive pattern mimicking the metal exterior of a laptop. Open it, and there's the screen and keyboard; open the next leaf, and there's a cut-out mouse."

In addition, spector cut+paste's Designer decided that they should not use only one typeface, because the typeface should reflect on the content of the text. This is demonstrated well in Issue 3, where every contribution has its own typeface.

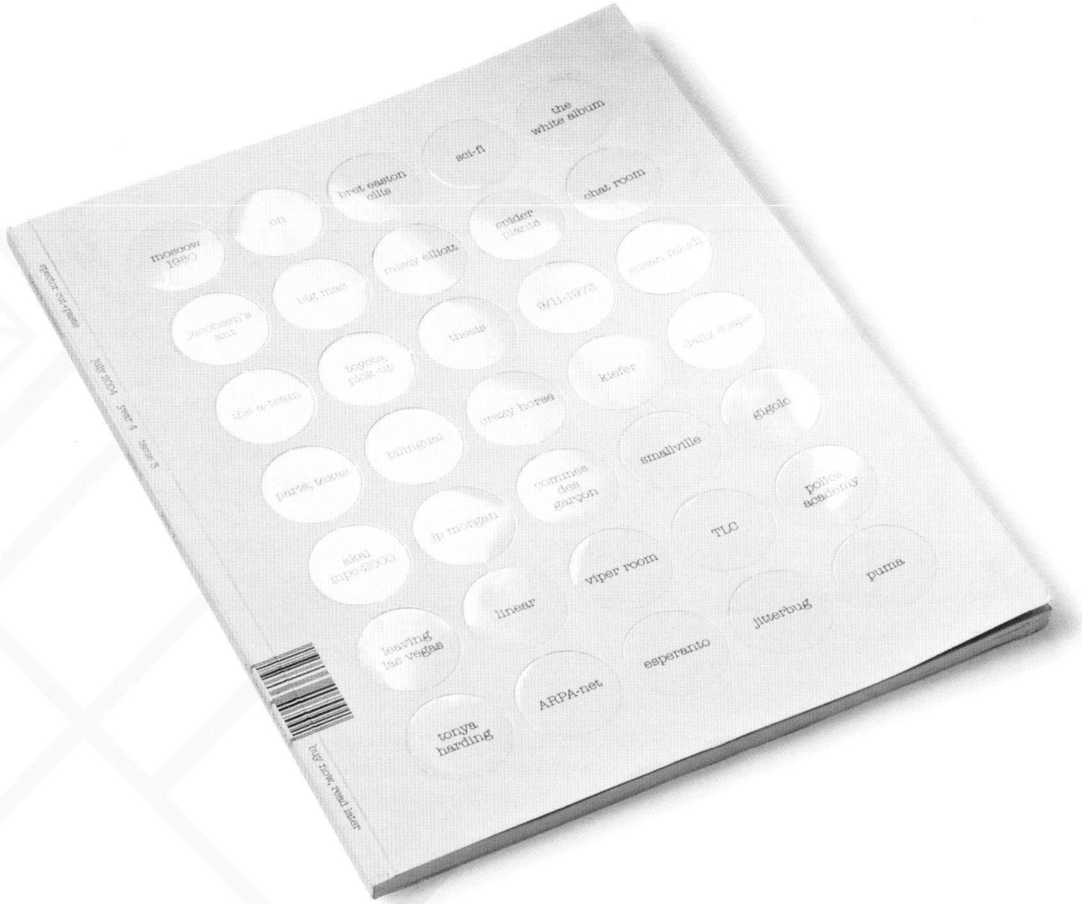

spector
cut+paste
MODEL
PHOTO/AUDIO
THE CONTINGENT
FOOTBALL/ART
SUBJECT/PRODUCT
LINK
REMAKE

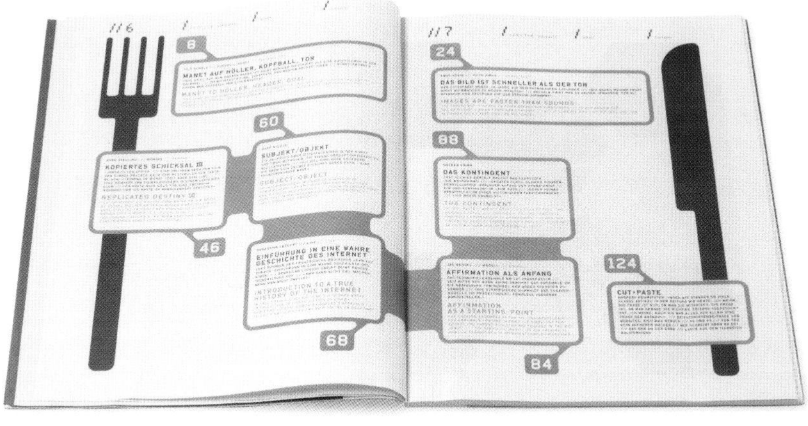
MANET AUF HÖLLER, KOPFBALL, TOR
DAS BILD IST SCHNELLER ALS DER TON
SUBJEKT/OBJEKT
KOPIERTES SCHICKSAL
DAS KONTINGENT
AFFIRMATION ALS ANFANG
CUT+PASTE

Art Direction: **Giampietro & Smith/ Stella Bugbee**
Publishers: **David Haskell (Editor-in-Chief)/Mohit Bhende (Executive Director)**
Country: **USA**

Topic

Topic was founded in 2001 by two Gates Scholars at Cambridge University, UK—David Haskell and Mohit Bhende—and is now published in New York. Its mission is to educate its readers by introducing them to a collection of individuals whose lives intersect with a chosen topic in a unique, provocative way. It restricts itself to first-person narratives and contemporary photography, and aims to allow individuals to speak in their own voices, to offer stories that are immediate, personal, and honest, and to democratize the idea of literary journalism. From the beginning, Haskell was eager to make the first-person contributions feel as substantial and literary as anything a serious journalist would write, but he was also clear that Topic is not a literary journal. He wanted it to be fresh and surprising, to be an active, engaging experience with a strong visual component.

Topic has an intimate, more contemplative way of thinking about the world than many other publications. Specific themes are explored in an interesting, varied way through the work of a number of contributors. According to the publishers, the magazine is about "taking a journey with some very distinctive travelers."
It has featured the work of a number of photographers and artists, including Taryn Simon, Richard Misrach, Justine Kurland, Phil Toledano, and Kai Regan.

In terms of design, the art directors want to make the magazine legible and readable, and to give it a youthful, but serious feel. "A lot of our problem-solving for Topic has been figuring out how to integrate words and pictures in an innovative way," explains Creative Director Rob Giampietro. "We want the pictures to speak to a reader on first glance and communicate a lot of the magazine's youthful approach and attitude. Then the words must follow through on the promise the images make."

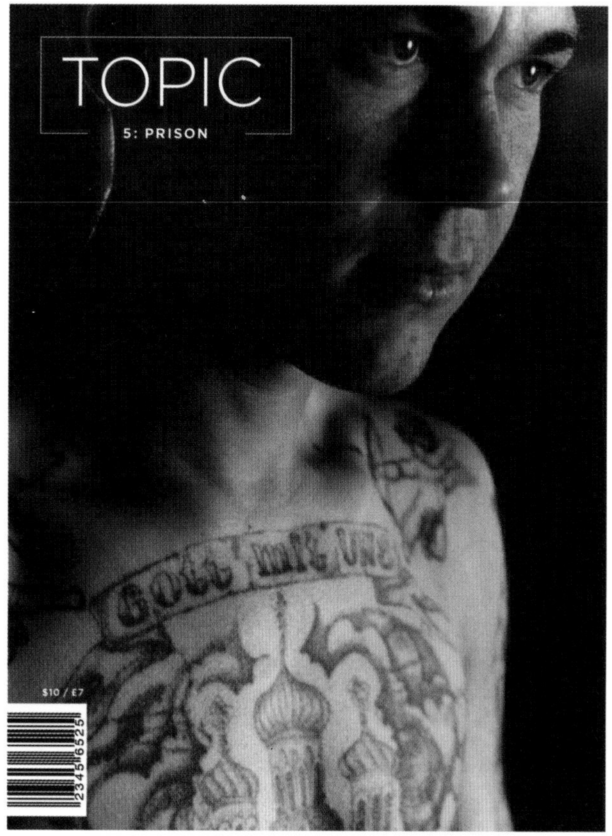

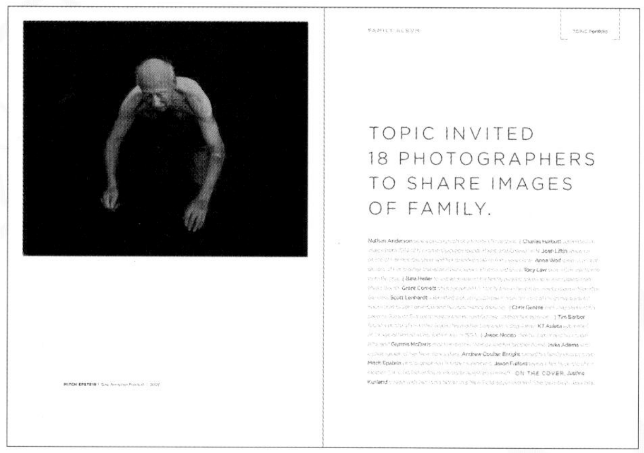

TOPIC
$8 / £5 / ♣12 / €8
topicmag.com
One should judge a man mainly from his depravities. —KLAUS KINSKI
ISSUE 8:
Sin
Owen King drinks underage, a Social Masturbator finds friends, and a Horny Mormon gets laid
PLUS Confessions by a Jewel Thief, a Fox Hunter, a Car Salesman and more!

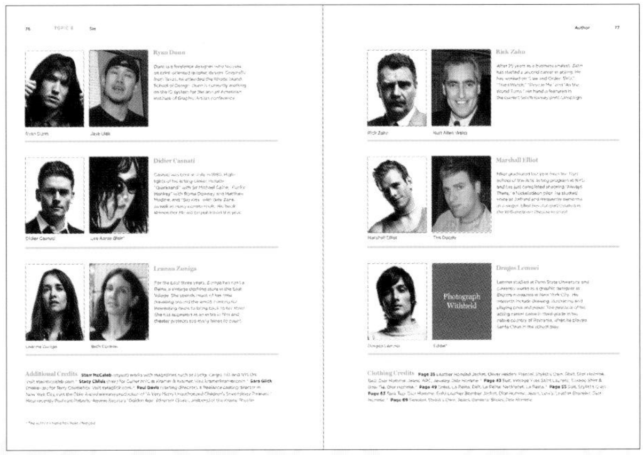

CANNIBALISM
Final Respects

Art Direction: **Sacha Spencer Trace**
Publisher: **Marmalade Magazine Ltd.**
Country: **UK**

Marmalade

Marmalade magazine was founded in 2002 to "fill a huge, gaping gap in the market for a magazine that celebrated creativity as a lifestyle choice," explains Art Director Sacha Spencer Trace. The intention is also to innovate and entertain.

Each issue uses the same fonts and grid in a very rigid format, which allows for experimentation with "materials" featured in each issue. When Issue 9, which celebrated new underground music, was put together it was the period when indie/alternative bands were starting to get attention, proving to the wider culture that underground and low-budget could also be mainstream and successful.

Therefore, the materials chosen were those that a fanzine would have used in the 1980s: photocopied and faxed pages, fluoro tape, and colored paper—altogether a raw and dirty look.

Issue 14 marked a redesign for Marmalade. After three years in production, and having reached sales of 50,000 copies per issue, the publishers and designers felt that it was time to evolve. The magazine was increased in size, the grid was changed, and through its design, Issue 14 aimed to explore the technique of collage in a subtle and understated way.

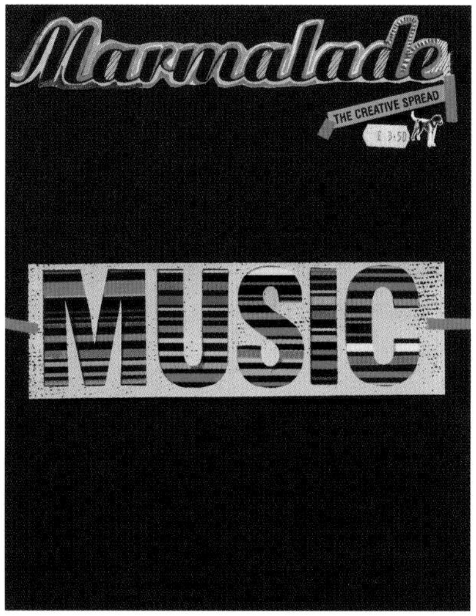

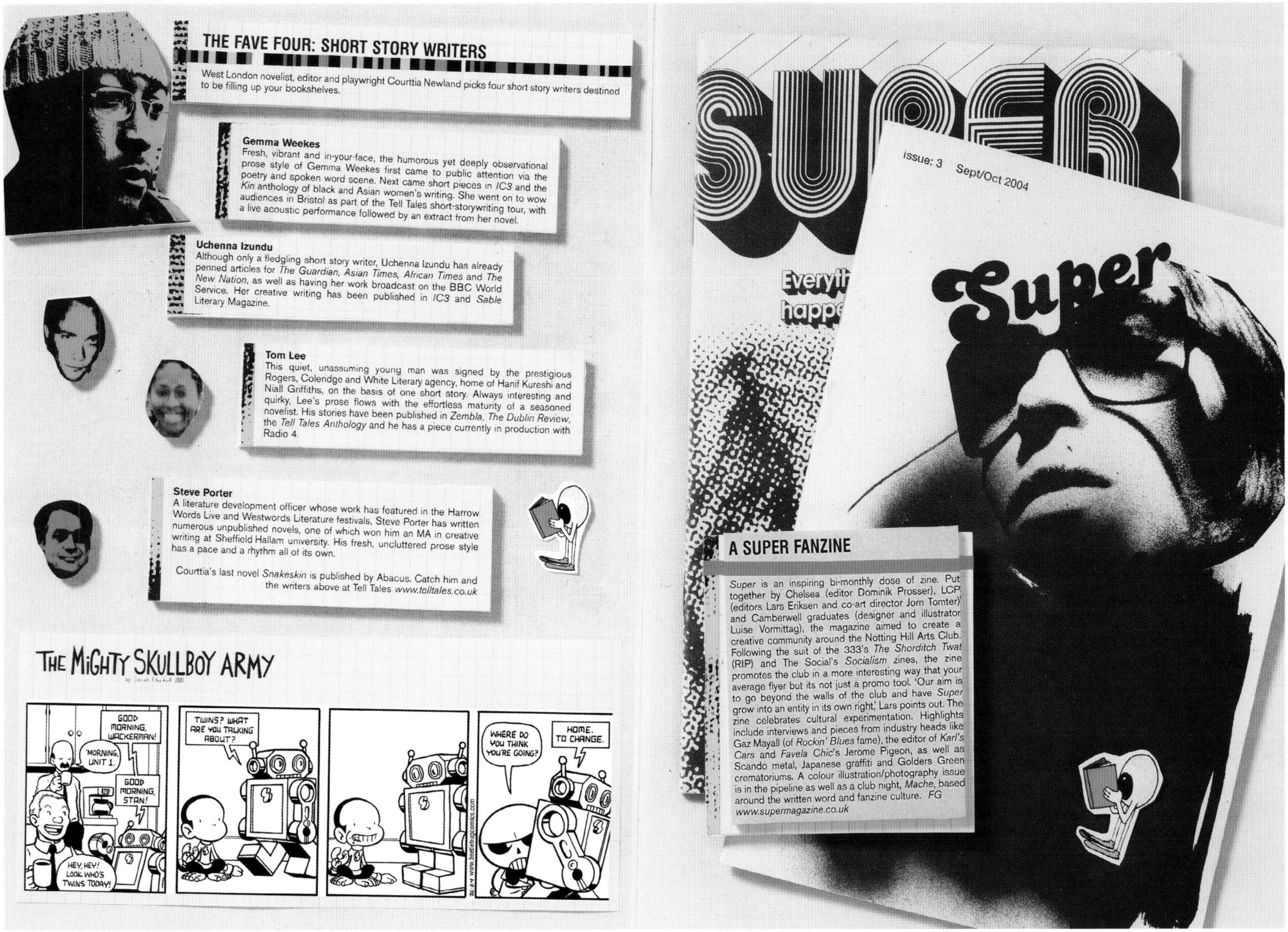

THE FAVE FOUR: SHORT STORY WRITERS

West London novelist, editor and playwright Courttia Newland picks four short story writers destined to be filling up your bookshelves.

Gemma Weekes
Fresh, vibrant and in-your-face, the humorous yet deeply observational prose style of Gemma Weekes first came to public attention via the poetry and spoken word scene. Next came short pieces in *IC3* and the *Kin* anthology of black and Asian women's writing. She went on to wow audiences in Bristol as part of the Tell Tales short-storywriting tour, with a live acoustic performance followed by an extract from her novel.

Uchenna Izundu
Although only a fledgling short story writer, Uchenna Izundu has already penned articles for *The Guardian, Asian Times, African Times* and *The New Nation*, as well as having her work broadcast on the BBC World Service. Her creative writing has been published in *IC3* and *Sable* Literary Magazine.

Tom Lee
This quiet, unassuming young man was signed by the prestigious Rogers, Coleridge and White Literary agency, home of Hanif Kureshi and Niall Griffiths, on the basis of one short story. Always interesting and quirky, Lee's prose flows with the effortless maturity of a seasoned novelist. His stories have been published in *Zembla, The Dublin Review*, the *Tell Tales Anthology* and he has a piece currently in production with Radio 4.

Steve Porter
A literature development officer whose work has featured in the Harrow Words Live and Westwords Literature festivals, Steve Porter has written numerous unpublished novels, one of which won him an MA in creative writing at Sheffield Hallam university. His fresh, uncluttered prose style has a pace and a rhythm all of its own.

Courttia's last novel *Snakeskin* is published by Abacus. Catch him and the writers above at Tell Tales *www.telltales.co.uk*

A SUPER FANZINE

Super is an inspiring bi-monthly dose of zine. Put together by Chelsea (editor Dominik Prosser), LCP (editors Lars Eriksen and co-art director Jorn Tomter) and Camberwell graduates (designer and illustrator Luise Vormittag), the magazine aimed to create a creative community around the Notting Hill Arts Club. Following the suit of the 333's *The Shorditch Twat* (RIP) and The Social's *Socialism* zines, the zine promotes the club in a more interesting way that your average flyer but its not just a promo tool. 'Our aim is to go beyond the walls of the club and have *Super* grow into an entity in its own right,' Lars points out. The zine celebrates cultural experimentation. Highlights include interviews and pieces from industry heads like Gaz Mayall (of *Rockin' Blues* fame), the editor of *Karl's Cars* and *Favela Chic*'s Jerome Pigeon, as well as Scando metal, Japanese graffiti and Golders Green crematoriums. A colour illustration/photography issue is in the pipeline as well as a club night, *Mache*, based around the written word and fanzine culture. *FG*
www.supermagazine.co.uk

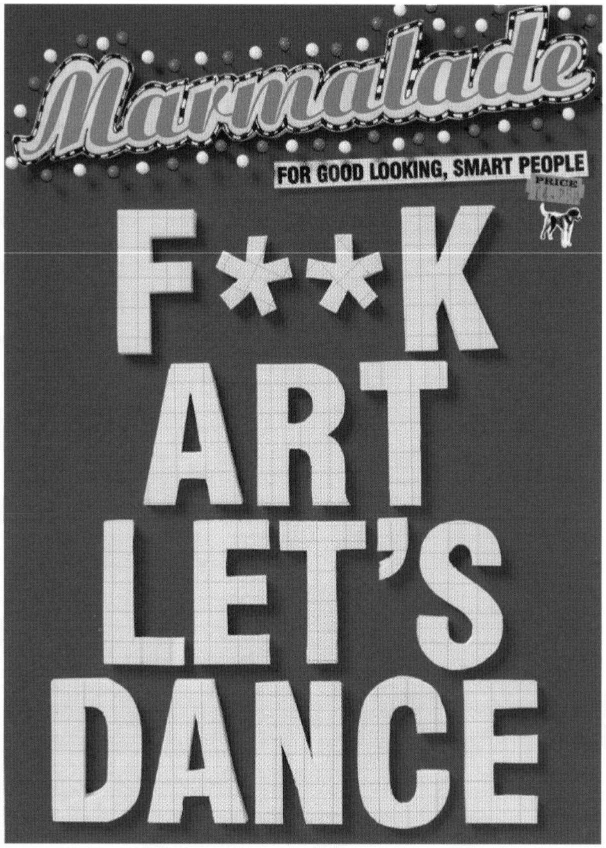
Marmalade
FOR GOOD LOOKING, SMART PEOPLE
F**K
ART
LET'S
DANCE

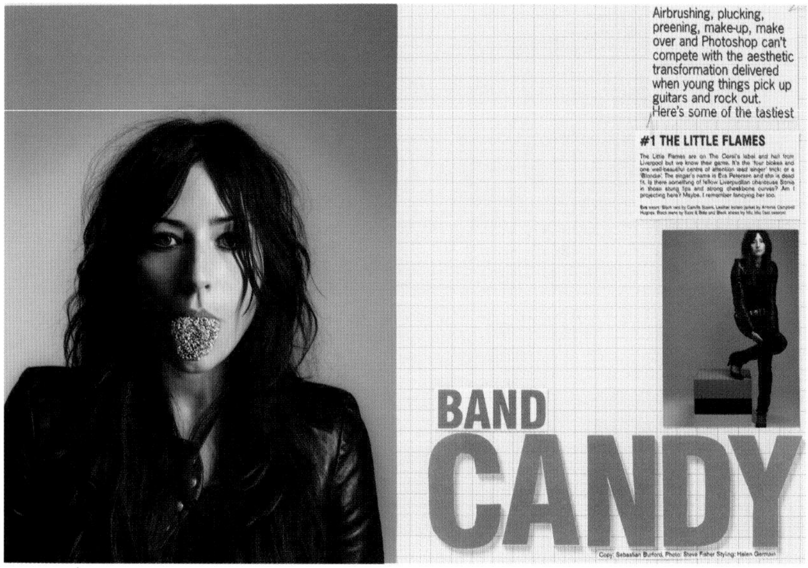
Airbrushing, plucking, preening, make-up, make over and Photoshop can't compete with the aesthetic transformation delivered when young things pick up guitars and rock out. Here's some of the tastiest
#1 THE LITTLE FLAMES
BAND
CANDY

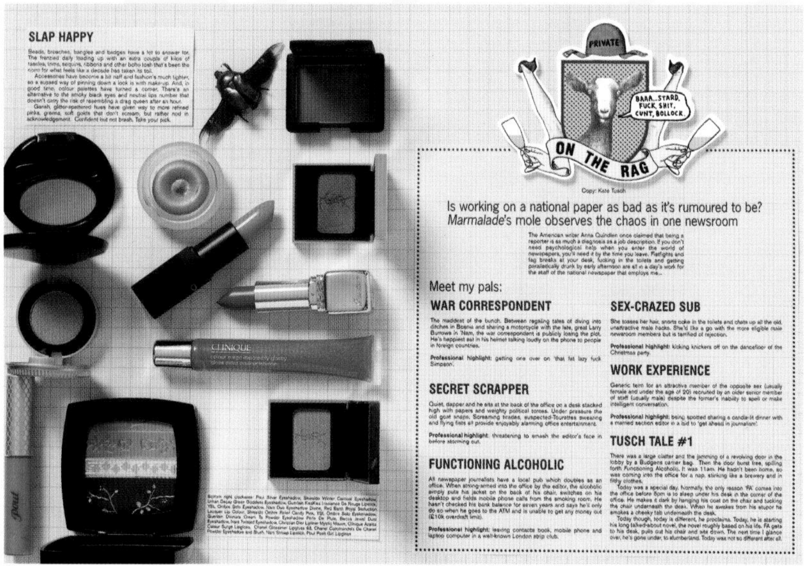
SLAP HAPPY
PRIVATE
ON THE RAG
Is working on a national paper as bad as it's rumoured to be?
Marmalade's mole observes the chaos in one newsroom
Meet my pals:
WAR CORRESPONDENT
SECRET SCRAPPER
FUNCTIONING ALCOHOLIC
SEX-CRAZED SUB
WORK EXPERIENCE
TUSCH TALE #1

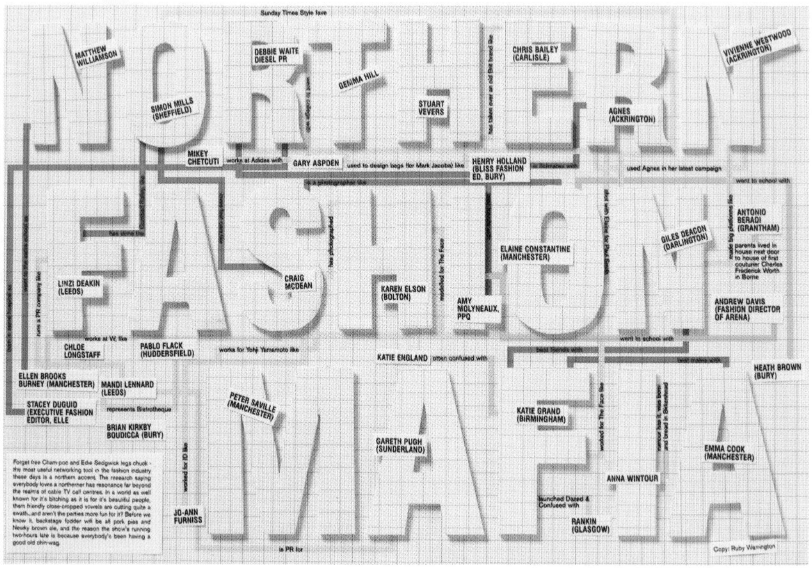
NORTHERN
FASHION
MAFIA

Ezra Petronio, Art Director, self service

Which are your three favorite magazine covers and why?
It is hard to pinpoint a specific cover, but rather some key revolutionary moments. The different styles that have impacted on us the most were the conceptual and elegant covers of the late Henry Wolf for Show magazine and Harper's Bazaar in the 1960s and 1970s. This was editorial art direction in its purest form, in the sense that he used all the ingredients available to illustrate editorial meaning. The early i-D covers were groundbreaking in that they introduced and celebrated individual style and street culture; they were socially very significant for that era. Finally, I must add all of Herb Lubalin's purely typographic and photographic work on the U & lc covers.

What is the key to art directing a magazine?
The ability to combine words and images to convey meaning. A good magazine has a balance of visual expression and stimulating articles; it documents expression and emotion.

Which other magazine would you most like to art direct?
I would find it challenging to explore editorial art direction within contexts or at a pace that is radically different from fashion and luxury. Working within the newspaper world could be one example, or art directing an underwater photoshoot with David Doubilet for National Geographic would be inspiring.

How do you approach each issue of self service?
Each issue starts as a reaction to the current situation and builds from there. What we're searching for is emotion. Once we have decided on our creative and editorial intentions, we usually start by commissioning about 20 photographic stories as well as over a dozen interviews. As images and words come in we work organically from there, altering and producing more. It is a very long and meticulous process guided by pure instinct.

Who do you work with to create each issue?
We always work with people who take the time to think about what they are doing and who will produce work that captures a sense of emotion. Contributors vary in their level of experience. Stylists include Anna Cockburn, Joe McKenna, Suzanne Koller, Jane How, Desiree Heiss, Camille Bidault-Waddington, or Chloë Sevigny, among others. Photographers include the likes of David Sims, Juergen Teller, Inez van Lamsweerde, Alasdair McLellan. There have been so many that have impacted on the soul of self service that it is hard to list.

There are more and more really creative, well-designed magazines being published for niche markets. Do you see this as the future of magazine publishing?
I don't think that the independent magazine is a modern concept. I have been waiting for some sort of radical magazine, but people want immediate success and gratification. We are living at a time when there is an acceleration of pace, an addiction to novelty, massive growth in fashion, music, and media, and an oversaturation of imagery. The problem is that a lot of people who have independent titles use them to promote their own egos. I don't want to be negative, but they have lost track of what they are about. Everything is cyclical, so I am sure in a few years we will be challenged by a whole new generation.

Which is your favorite magazine, one you collect?
I buy so many magazines, and keep them as archives more than as a collection. We have started putting together a very big collection of old magazines, thanks to eBay.

Colin Metcalf, Art Director, GUM

Which are your three favorite magazine covers of all time?
Avant Garde Magazine, Issue 7, from 1969, which featured a fantastic twist on the American Revolutionary War painting The Spirit of '76. Although photographed, the cover has the painterly atmosphere of the original icon, and the suggestively clad female drummer, the black drummer, and hippie flutist embody the sexual and racial revolution happening in the late 1960s. The Time magazine from May 1945 that featured a painting of Hitler's face on a white background, with a bloody, red "X" painted over it. It's completely startling in its simplicity, and conveys without any text the violent satisfaction that his demise evoked. Rudy VanderLans' early editions of Emigre always had memorable, iconic covers that broke the conventional wisdom regarding publication design. I think our favorite issue is the Rick Valicenti-designed cover from 1993 that featured a solid field of electric blue with a vertical "hot-rod" flame in yellow, orange, and red. It was totally hypnotic. All of these covers really are about a single, potent image unfettered by competing type and information.

What is the key to art directing a magazine?
Focus and consistency. It's important to set a well-defined color palette and some core guidelines for the visual vocabulary you use. There's always the temptation to pursue every clever idea you generate, but at the end of the day, you have to edit quite a lot. The magazine that looks like an effortless, complete thought usually is the product of a pretty disciplined approach and thorough attention to lots of details.

Which other magazine would you most like to art direct?
Right now we really just want to design for our own content and editorial. So I don't know if there is another publication that would come to mind. It's really about the overall authorship.

What is the story behind GUM magazine?
In 2001 Kevin [Grady] was Design Director for the Truth Campaign—an anti-tobacco-industry campaign—and I was Art Directing RES, the film-company magazine, and both of us were ready for a change. We wanted to get back to creating something very personal. We knew that it would ultimately be a publication and that it'd be very fun and pop oriented, but we evolved the content and the format with a lot of experimentation. We almost had our hopes dashed when 9/11 happened, because we believed that our particular vision would have no place in the immediate wake of such horrors. But, as months passed, we found that just the opposite was true. GUM was definitely sugary, fun, and accessible, but it was something comparatively intelligent in a field of fashion-driven vacuousness, and people seemed to want that.

What inspires the creative idea behind each issue?
GUM has been described, aptly, as a blog with extraordinary production values. We follow the thread of whatever interests us at the moment. Usually, there are some common themes rattling around, and then we collaborate with people who are gifted writers, photographers, and illustrators to bring it all to life. So the process becomes almost like a controlled experiment. GUM is actually a stand-alone piece of art created with the cooperation and passion of a group of very motivated artists.

How do you approach each issue?
Kevin will come up with a packaging concept, I'll develop typography and visual conventions, and we'll develop some content ideas together. We both write a fair bit, and when you start sharing your thoughts with the other contributors, it really starts to evolve. For instance, with GUM2, writer Rob Bundy always wanted to interview Ray Bradbury, so he made that

connection happen. It turned out that photographer Guido Vitti had some concepts based on stories from The Martian Chronicles, which he went ahead and shot. Then Kevin created an intro based on Fahrenheit 451, and suddenly you have this beautiful visual narrative to accompany the written piece, and it's all an act of improvisation. Once you embark with intention, the issue starts to weave itself to some degree. Then the final stages involve a lot of back and forth between Kevin and I about the ultimate formatting, design, and whatnot.

Who do you work with to create GUM?
We work with a fairly consistent group of people. Guido Vitti, Jeanne Hilary (photographers), Robert Bundy, and Jim Marcus (writers) have contributed to both issues, and will probably be in GUM3 as well. On GUM2, we worked with painter/illustrator Greg Ruhl to create the cover art, comic-book art, and several spreads inside. But each issue involves the work of a solid 15 people in some way or another.

What is important about the team that you work with?
That there be a synergy in both creativity and attitude. It's almost like being in a band. You have to trust that your partners in the process are great at what they do, that they'll put their best effort forth, and that they're not selfishly motivated beyond what's normal. We have a great group of friends and collaborators, so we don't have many issues like that.

How important do you think the cover image on a magazine is and why? What makes a good one or bad one?
Extremely important. When we interviewed Chip Kidd and John Spencer in GUM, the premise that began our discussion was that CD packaging really influences how you hear the music. It's not rational, but it makes emotional sense and it's just plain true. To an extent, the same is true with a book jacket or a magazine cover. All things equal on the pages between, a good cover design heightens your overall perception. One thing it can't do, though, is make up for a mediocre product. So the excellent cover has to really reflect values throughout the whole publication. As for what makes a good or bad cover, I don't think that can be so easily quantified. But I know that we're suckers for Flaunt. The covers are always amazing.

There are more and more really creative, well-designed magazines being published for niche markets. Do you see this as the future of magazine publishing?
Yeah, probably. A lot of people think that everything will evaporate into Web publishing. But people like the physical artifact. It's tactile, and portable, and personal, and we don't think that will ever go away completely. It's certainly true that we live in an age of proliferating niches, which, ironically, is entirely the product of the Web. If you can target your niche fairly specifically, and those people know where they can find you, it makes the notion of a sustainable little niche business actually tenable. But the economics of publishing are not very charitable, so you still have to be pretty practical and savvy to build long-term success.

Which is your favorite magazine, one that you always collect?
We don't have any contemporary magazines that we always collect, but Ralph Ginzburg's Avant Garde, which ran from 1968 to 1971, is a favorite. Although it's been out of print for more than 30 years now, we're still trying to get a complete set. The covers in particular were always a complete visual experience, and that magazine is really a precursor and an influence for our new magazine, LEMON, which debuted in February 2006.

05

"The fourth and fifth words: paper and ink. Experimenting with different papers and printing techniques is a process in itself."

Giorgio De Mitri, Publisher, Editor, and Art Director, CUBE

Printing & Finishing

"The whole area of magazine publishing is fragmenting. Within the next 20 years we will have a workable version of e-paper; it's going to be a difficult and exciting time for magazines."

Jonathan Barnbrook, Art Director and Designer, Kohkoku

Introduction

As magazine publishing becomes more experimental in terms of subject matter and content, so too do the printing and finishing techniques that art directors and designers employ for their titles. From uncoated stock to the use of spot varnishes, the ways in which designers can differentiate their titles are many and varied.

Today, more and more publishers, art directors, and designers are taking advantage of these and becoming increasingly creative with the production of their magazines. Some—Half Empty magazine, for example—include a selection of stickers with each issue as an "extra" gift for the reader, while soDA magazine includes pull-out posters that in one issue were carefully planted between French-folded pages. The inclusion of small postcards or small removable pictures is also common. Other titles—SHERBERT is one—come with hand-printed covers or use embossing on the covers and die-cut details both inside and out.

Whatever the printing technique or finish may be, it is the extra consideration involved in executing these interesting or unusual touches that makes the reader feel like they are buying something more than a disposable item that will sit on their coffee table for only a couple of weeks. These elements add value and a sense of the unique to a publication, and help turn them from throwaway items into something the reader wants to keep and treasure. Like a good book, these very niche titles become collectible, talked about, and recommended.

Art Direction: **Oneil Edwards/Chetan Mangat** (for issues shown here)
Publisher: **Devon Dikeou**
Country: **USA**

zingmagazine

New York–based Devon Dikeou was a practicing contemporary artist when she set up zingmagazine in 1995. As she explains, "I was making artwork that provoked the participation of an audience, and I was very much interested in this idea of the space that existed between the artwork, the audience, and the gallery, and not editing that experience, or lack thereof. The magazine came directly out of that.

To this end, Dikeou and her team gave between 10 and 16 pages of each issue to a featured artist or creative, letting them determine the nature of what would be published in each of their "curated" sections. This has been a distinctive feature of zingmagazine, so each issue is unique. "Initially, the magazine was printed black-and-white, but it is now color. However, we've always printed on matte paper," adds Dikeou. "Now both matte paper and black-and-white printing proliferate in the printed world of both art and fashion publications, and are embraced as design vision rather than seen as a design or cost flaw."

Images featured are chosen by the curators themselves, who also choose or generate an appropriate typeface to reflect and support their concept. "Our only design elements that are not a pure reflection of the curators are our front and back covers," explains Dikeou. "Originally, letter correspondences of different historical noteworthies were featured on the cover, but now we use stock photographic images that conjure up the essence of the letter chosen for each issue with the letters themselves now featured on the back cover."

The idea for this cover concept was to democratize the importance of each curated project. By early 2006 zingmagazine had published or produced over 300 curated projects encompassing 6,000 pages, including eight books, four posters, five music CDs, and two unisex fashion satchels.

Archibald
MacLeish

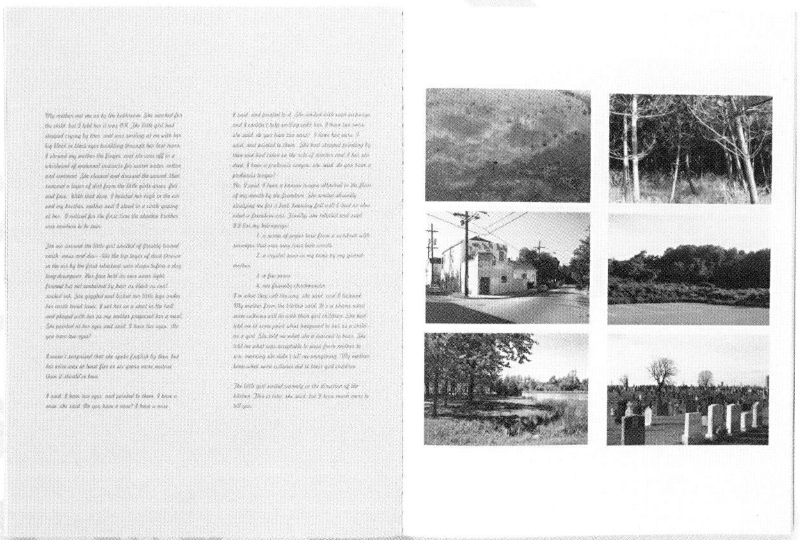

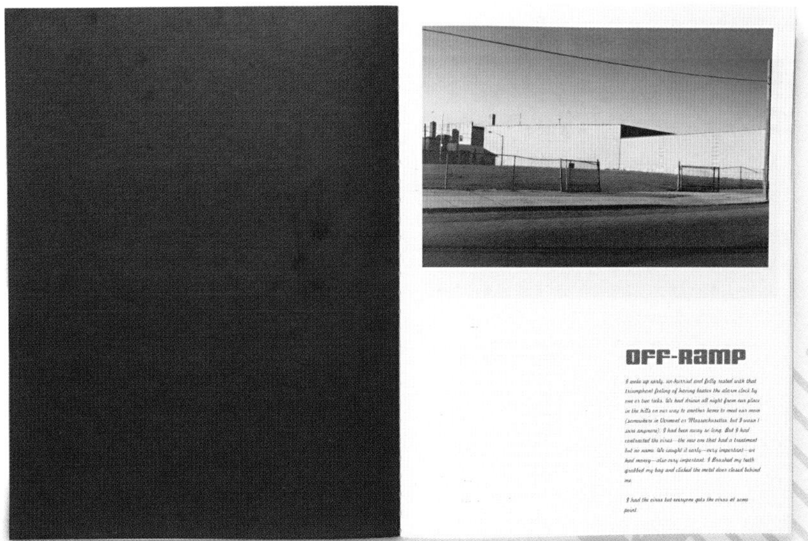
OFF-RAMP

soDA #27 «A plan is a plan»
Am Anfang war der Plan – visionär, euphorisch.
So, da ist was. Der Plan einfach wie kompliziert:
soDA bricht auf und begibt sich für die nächsten
drei Ausgaben auf Reisen – strebt gegen den fernen
Osten, gegen den unbekannten Westen und in die
mythische Stadt Fès. +++ Specials: Weltkarte + Kofferaufkleber

Art Direction: **Various**
Creative Direction: **Martin Lötscher**
Publisher: **Martin Lötscher/Iris Ruprecht**
Country: **Switzerland**

soDA

The founders of soDA wanted to confront existing magazine formats with something individual and more suited to meeting their creative requirements when they came up with the idea for their magazine in 1996. This they did, and soon after soDA gained public recognition, being described as "refreshingly different."

Shown here is Issue 27. The thematic focus of all the magazines in 2005 was travel, and with this particular issue the publishers wanted to gain insight into the destinations they planned to travel to that year, naming the issue A Plan Is a Plan. "Generally speaking, we create the concept and the themes of the issues beforehand and then search for contributors," explains Iris Ruprecht. "We look for people that have something to say about the subject we have chosen for an issue."

This issue is beautifully produced, with an outer debossed cream cover and contrasting pink belly band. Inside sits the magazine along with a map and stickers. The magazine is printed on uncoated stock, save for the high-gloss inserted images, and features many pullouts.

(See page 37 for Issue 21 of soDA.)

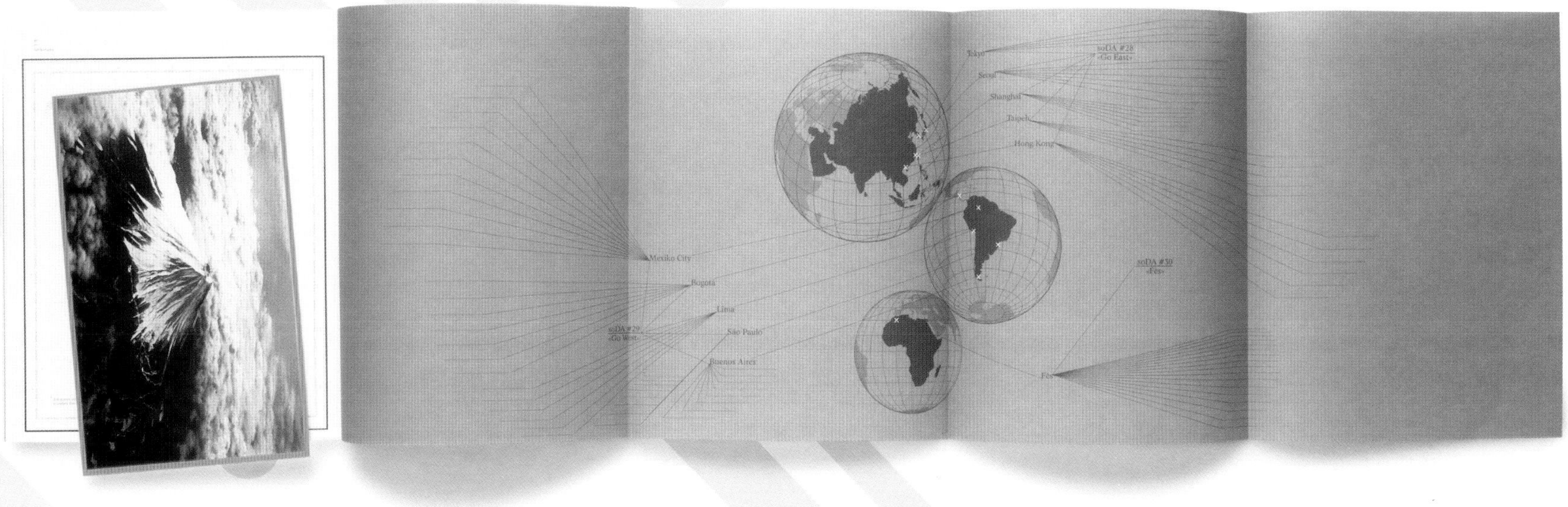
Tokyo
Seoul
Shanghai
Taipeh
Hong Kong
soDA #28
«Go East»
Mexiko City
Bogota
Lima
São Paulo
Buenos Aires
soDA #29
«Go West»
soDA #30
«Fes»

REA-
LI-
SIE-
RUNG

PLAN

Art Direction: **Kevin Grady/ Colin Metcalf (GUM)**
Publisher: **GUM**
Country: **USA**

LEMON

LEMON is the sister publication of GUM magazine, created by US team Kevin Grady and Colin Metcalf. Issue 1 (shown here) came out in February 2006, and it is published every six months. "Ralph Ginzburg's Avant Garde Magazine, which ran from 1968 to 1971, is the ultimate inspiration behind the size and typography we chose for LEMON," explains Metcalf. "We wanted to create a more mainstream vehicle for the GUM sensibility that would also make sense to a few like-minded sponsors. We also skewed the personality of LEMON a little more toward the glamorous. So far, we've been able to use a more subtle sponsorship model, rather than a traditional page-advertising model. This integrates the advertising more seamlessly into the content, which is good for the sponsors' images and good for the overall coherence of the magazine."

For this launch issue, Guido Vitti shot the front cover and Dave Bradley shot the back. It also features the work of Norwegian student Ronja Svenning Berge. As a tip of the hat to Ginzburg's magazine, the LEMON team modified Avant Garde for the headline face, by creating alternate characters with sharp angles. For the body copy they sought out a restrained serif face with plenty of character, deciding on Alias Union by Gareth Hague. The cover was printed on a high-gloss sheet, with a matte-laminate treatment and a spot aqueous varnish giving it a sumptuous finish. On the yellow insert cards they used a lemon-scented varnish on a matte-coated sheet as a scratch-and-sniff feature.

(See page 20 for Issue 1 of GUM.)

THE PRESENCE
THE PRESENCE
THE PRESENCE

NEW COLUMN
The Real JT
Saber-Toothed Mommas
BY JT LEROY
'Supernatural love is the desire for life to go on.'
WARHOLIAN DE

Art Direction: **The Kitchen**
Publisher: **Graphite Media**
Country: **UK**

The End

The End is one of London's most popular clubs. In 2005 London-based designers The Kitchen were asked by The End to put together a fanzine-style publication for the club, featuring articles about the DJs that play there, club nights, and lifestyle. There was no design brief as such, but The Kitchen was asked to create a publication that did not look like something produced for a club.

Simplicity became the key to the design, with most of the fanzine printed in two colors. This makes it a magazine that has a fuss-free, classic feel to it. The cover image is an illustration by UK artist Will Barras. It has been printed using foil block in blue, which is set off well against the grayboard it is printed on. The magazine is extremely rich visually, packed with a variety of illustrations of the featured DJs, created by, among others, David Walker, Sam Green, and Joel Clifford.

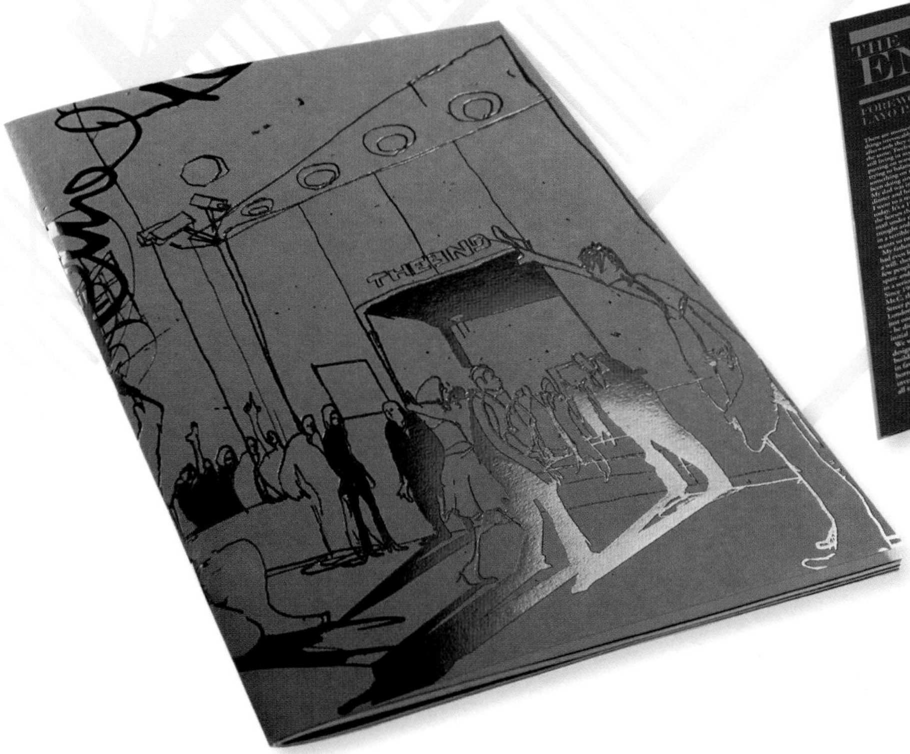

Art Direction: **BB/Saunders**
Design: **BB/Saunders**
Publisher: **Warren Beeby/ Andrew G. Hobbs**
Country: **UK**

Centrefold

Centrefold was originally conceived as a selling tool for one individual photographer, Andrew G. Hobbs, but soon grew beyond that into a magazine in its own right, featuring work from other contributors. The magazine is made up of a series of interleaved pages—or "posters"—that feature the work of young image-making talent. It is designed to work as a sequence, like any other publication, but also allows each "centerfold" to be removed from the publication to exist outside of the context in which it was originally placed.

"Sometimes the images on these pages are completed by viewing them as posters, and others are deconstructed or cut in half to appear with other images or graphics in the magazine," explains Designer Martin Saunders. "The idea is intended to be playful, and presents endless possibilities with each new issue. I've always been fascinated by images that have been removed from magazines to be displayed elsewhere, giving them another life away from the original publication."

It is of a larger format, is unbound, and is limited to a print run of only 500 copies, which are distributed in selected bookstores and galleries. Photographer Andrew Hobbs has been the main contributor, but Centrefold has also included the work of Mario Godlewski, Tony Gibson, Julie Bentley, and Chris Turner.

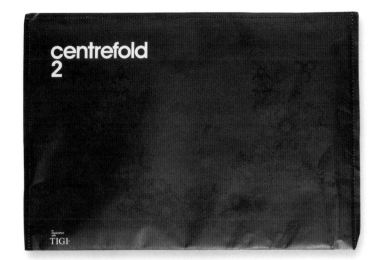

Art Direction: **Warren Jackson (Fifty-One)**
Design: **Warren Jackson (Fifty-One)**
Publisher: **John Brown Citrus Publishing**
Country: **UK**

Carlos

Carlos is Virgin Atlantic's in-flight magazine for its Upper Class cabin passengers. The brief from Virgin Atlantic to Art Director Warren Jackson and his team was to "reflect Virgin Atlantic's philosophy of innovation," and the magazine's distinctive design sees a departure from the normal glossy newsstand format of the majority of in-flight magazines. Its small format—oversized A5—uncoated brown-card cover with subtle use of spot varnish, off-white uncoated stock for the inside pages, and pale-blue typeface all make for a lo-fi, but classy publication with an edge.

When first published it was quickly picked up by British Vogue as a must-have, and has since become a much talked about, difficult to get publication. "With Carlos we wanted to provoke the idea in the passenger that they were part of a 'club,'" explains Jackson, "that they had stumbled across this fanzine-style, literary 'scrapbook' belonging to a fictional man called Carlos and they were to become privy to his thoughts, whimsies, and interests."

Carlos contains no photography at all—except on the advertisers' pages, which also use a glossy stock—and is made up solely of hand-created illustrations. The covers have all been by the artist Jonathan Schofield, and the inside pages have featured the work of Stanley Donwood, Holly Johnson, and Johan Malkovich as well as texts by Woody Allen, Pete Robinson, and Truman Capote. What is also unusual is that there is no Virgin Atlantic branding in the publication. The typefaces used are Mrs Eaves family, Hoefler Text family, and occasionally Helvetica for spoof classified ads.

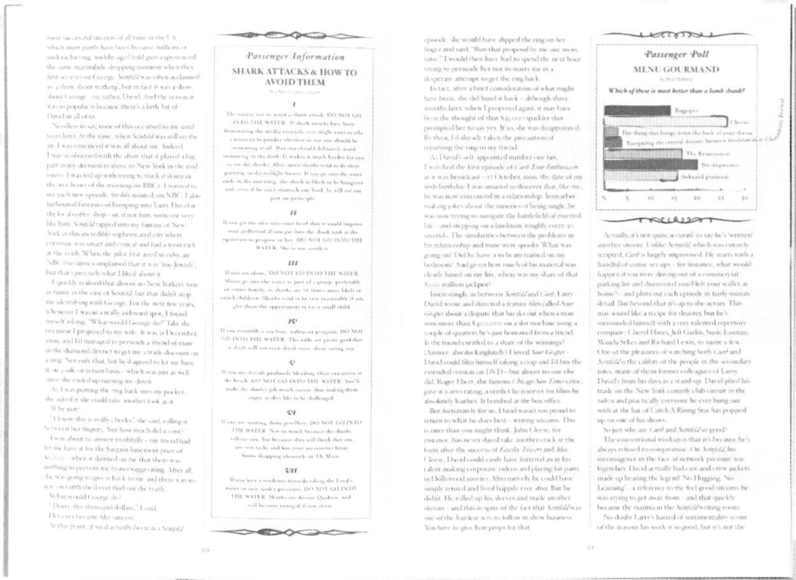
Passenger Information
SHARK ATTACKS & HOW TO AVOID THEM
Passenger Poll
MENU GOURMAND

45
WILDE CHILD
MORRISSEY

GIRLS:
NEW ORLEANS

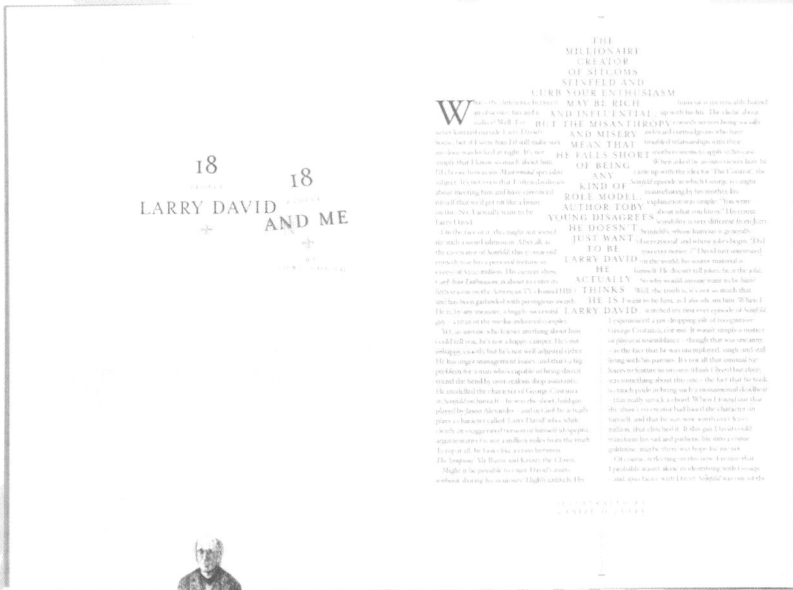
18
LARRY DAVID
18
AND ME
THE MILLIONAIRE CREATOR OF SITCOMS SEINFELD AND CURB YOUR ENTHUSIASM MAY BE RICH AND INFLUENTIAL BUT THE MISANTHROPY AND MISERY MEAN THAT HE FALLS SHORT OF BEING ANY KIND OF ROLE MODEL. AUTHOR TOBY YOUNG DISAGREES. HE DOESN'T JUST WANT TO BE LARRY DAVID. HE ACTUALLY THINKS HE IS LARRY DAVID.

Art Direction: **Ralf Herms**
Publisher: **Ralf Herms**
Countries: **Germany/Austria**

+rosebud

+rosebud is published in Austria/Germany by Art Director and Editor Ralf Herms. Shown here is Issue 5, the theme of which was mystery. As for all issues of +rosebud, Herms decided on the theme and then invited people from a wide range of professions and disciplines—including artists, designers, and writers—to approach the topic and contribute their results.

He sent 200 prospective contributors a cassette called "Welcome to Mysteryland," which, when played, gave them the instructions for their task. Contributors include Kessler, Kellas, and Mayer, and, shown here, Chloe Potter, Timo Reger, austriancomfort, and Alexander Egger.

The printing and finishing of this issue, as with all issues of +rosebud, has been clearly thought through and perfectly executed. It is bound as a hardcover book, complete with blue page marker. The title and cover illustration have been foil-blocked on the black cover, making for a magazine that is solid and luxurious, in fact more like a book than a magazine, something you'd definitely want to keep and treasure.

When my father took us to the steam bath
for the first time
Fairytales
By Chloë Potter

36
advantage of being
a »rich man's wife.«
37

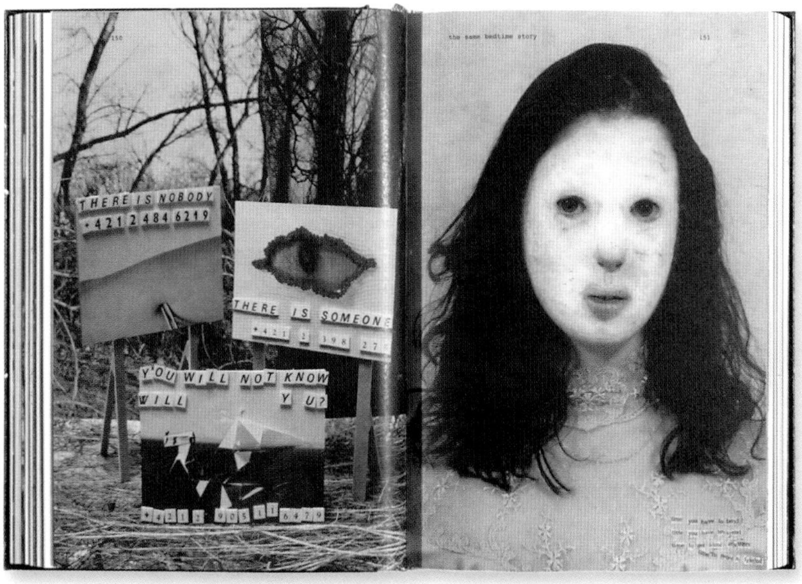
150
the same bedtime story
151
THERE IS NOBODY
+421 2 484 6219
THERE IS SOMEONE
YOU WILL NOT KNOW
WILL Y U?

126
a name out of an alphabetical list.
High pressure areas get male, whereas
127

Art Direction: **Dave Eggers/ Alvaro Villanueva**
Design: **Dave Eggers/Alvaro Villanueva**
Publisher: **Barb Bersche**
Country: **USA**

The Believer

The Believer is a world-renowned forum for books and book criticism. It provides an alternative to typical book reviews and aims to extend the ever-shortening shelf life of new books, revive interest in books long overlooked, and stress the interconnectivity between books pop culture, politics, art, and music. The magazine features essays on these topics, as well as lengthy interviews with philosophers, politicians, and rock musicians.

Designwise it also challenges the norms and deliberately tries to avoid overdesign and following trends. To this end the designers created an unusual, bold cover grid, with the illustrations of Charles Burns as its cornerstone and trademark, within which only the portraits, coverlines, and colors would change. The use of an uncoated stock and earthy colors is an attempt to emphasize that the magazine is meant to be kept and shelved, and not thrown away. The contents feature on the outside back cover, which is an unusual touch, and Bembo and Clarendon typefaces have been used throughout. In general, the focus of the design is the text, and it is beautifully laid out, with a classic "old-fashioned" esthetic.

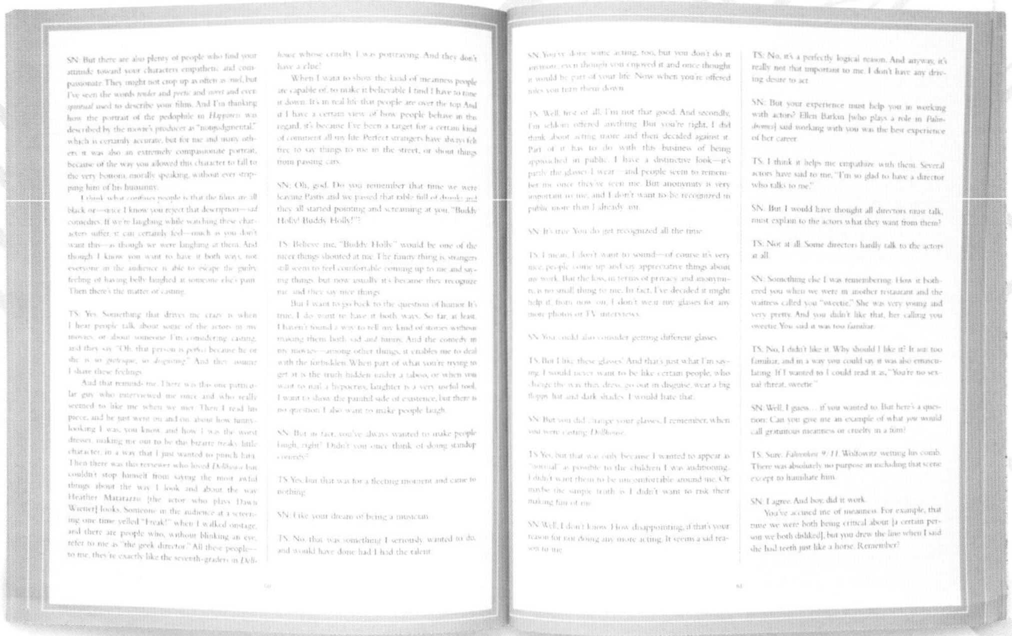

THE BELIEVER
FEBRUARY 2005
Vol. 3, No. 1
Zane Grey and the Borgias . . . . . Jim Shepard 3
An Era of Awkward Repression . . . . . Mark Oppenheimer 9
Paradise Poem . . . . . Dean Young 16
Underway . . . . . Various 18
More Sex, Please, I'm British . . . . . Mark Swartz 19
Why Look at Fish? . . . . . Ginger Strand 23
One-Page Reviews . . . . . Various 37
Whale Tale . . . . . Lawrence Krauser 43
Light: Marfa Mystery Light . . . . . Susan Briante 47
Conservative: Jim . . . . . Jon Mooallem 48
Paul Auster . . . . . in conversation with . . . . . Jonathan Lethem 49
Todd Solondz . . . . . interviewed by . . . . . Sigrid Nunez 58
Schema: Non-Essential Stock Photography . . . . . Brian McMullen & Chester 68
4-Color Comics: "Illustrations for My Novel" . . . . . Michael Kupperman 70
Eve Sussman . . . . . interviewed by . . . . . Suzanne Snider 71
Stuff I've Been Reading: A monthly column . . . . . Nick Hornby 81
La Zona Fantasma: A new monthly column . . . . . Javier Marías 85
THE BELIEVER
THE VISUAL ISSUE
Inside: A DVD with FILMS BY or ABOUT SPIKE JONZE, SELMA BLAIR, MIRANDA JULY, DAVID O. RUSSELL, PATTON OSWALT, HOVERCRAFTS, ET AL.
And: HACKING OLD NINTENDOS; TATTOO FICTION; JOHN BARTH on OLD BEGINNINGS; THE MALAYSIAN NEW-WAVE CINEMA; A LUSH ART INSERT CURATED BY ERIC FISCHL; MILK ADDICTION & THE BIRTH OF MODERNITY; LIFE MASKS OF THE FAMOUS AND THE DEAD
DEC 2005/JAN 2006 ★ $10

Art Direction: **Marty Spellerberg**
Editor: **Marty Spellerberg**
Publisher: **Marty Spellerberg**
Country: **Canada**

Half Empty

Half Empty magazine was originally founded as a Web site by Marty Spellerberg, James Paterson, and Emily Mets. The three were still in high school at the time. The original format consisted of a leading article on a main site each week, with Paterson's Flash section, "Sunday," and Mets' blog, "Dustgirl's Diary." When Paterson introduced a section called "Blink," the site started getting a lot of attention. "Blink" was a gallery of Flash animation, and it predated some of the larger, commercially backed projects, such as Hotwired's Animation Express.

In late 2002 they wanted to take the project to the next level, which meant print—specifically newsprint. "I knew the look of the thing before I started," explains Spellerberg. "I'd been using this ugly typeface called Elite online, and had already developed a style with it. It's monospaced and often mistaken for Courier, which is what gives it that lo-fi, 'zine feeling. Newsprint is fantastic, but not delicate, so I jammed the images up against each other and only used a couple of font sizes. I had a lot of cheap space to fill, which is how the headlines got to be so big."

Since then Half Empty has always been created for the publishers' own enjoyment. There is no advertising, which, as Spellerberg says, on the one hand keeps the project from really growing as it could, but on the other protects the creative priority. The printed annual takes the form of a newspaper, featuring artist and curator interviews, with much original art and illustration as well as a few added extras, such as stickers.

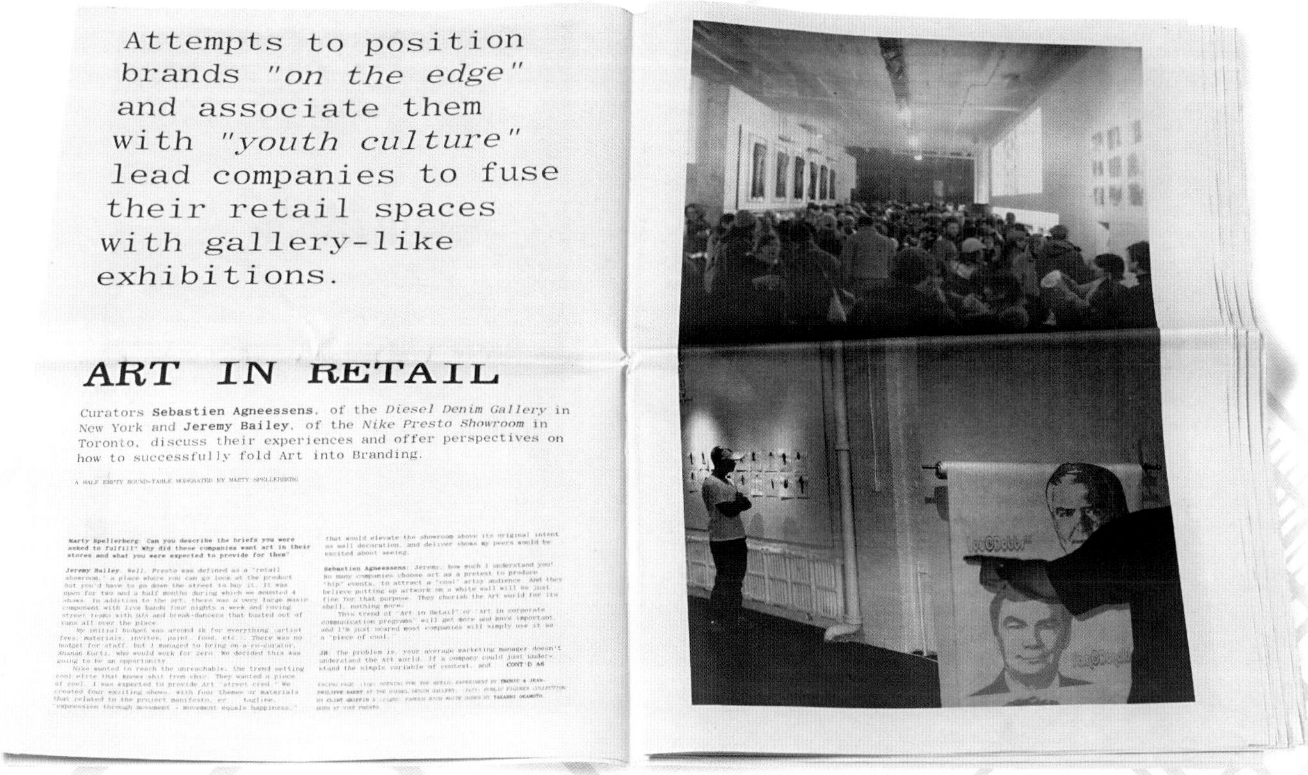

Attempts to position brands *"on the edge"* and associate them with *"youth culture"* lead companies to fuse their retail spaces with gallery-like exhibitions.

ART IN RETAIL

Curators **Sebastien Agneessens**, of the *Diesel Denim Gallery* in New York and **Jeremy Bailey**, of the *Nike Presto Showroom* in Toronto, discuss their experiences and offer perspectives on how to successfully fold Art into Branding.

A HALF EMPTY ROUND-TABLE MODERATED BY MARTY SPELLERBERG

Marty Spellerberg: Can you describe the briefs you were asked to fulfill? Why did these companies want art in their stores and what you were expected to provide for them?

Jeremy Bailey: Well, Presto was defined as a "retail showroom," a place where you can go look at the product but you'd have to go down the street to buy it. It was open for two and a half months during which we mounted 4 shows. In addition to the art, there was a very large music component with live bands four nights a week and roving street teams with DJs and break-dancers that busted out of vans all over the place.

My initial budget was around 4k for everything (artist fees, materials, invites, paint, food, etc.). There was no budget for staff, but I managed to bring on a co-curator, Shanan Kurtz, who would work for zero. We decided this was going to be an opportunity.

Nike wanted to reach the unreachable, the trend setting cool elite that knows shit from chic. They wanted a piece of cool. I was expected to provide Art "street cred." We created four exciting shows, with four themes or materials that related to the project manifesto, er... tagline, "expression through movement - movement equals happiness," that would elevate the showroom above its original intent as wall decoration, and deliver shows my peers would be excited about seeing.

Sebastien Agneessens: Jeremy, how much I understand you! So many companies choose art as a pretext to produce "hip" events, to attract a "cool" artsy audience. And they believe putting up artwork on a white wall will be just fine for that purpose. They cherish the Art world for its shell, nothing more.

This trend of "Art in Retail" or "Art in corporate communication programs" will get more and more important and I'm just scared most companies will simply use it as a "piece of cool."

JB: The problem is, your average marketing manager doesn't understand the Art world. If a company could just understand the simple variable of context, and **CONT'D A6**

FACING PAGE: (TOP) OPENING FOR THE RETAIL EXPERIMENT BY **TRONIC & JEAN-PHILIPPE BAERT** AT THE DIESEL DENIM GALLERY. (LEFT) PUBLIC FIGURES COLLECTION BY **CLINT GRIFFIN** & (RIGHT) FAMOUS RICH WHITE DUDES BY **TAKASHI OKAMOTO**. BOTH AT NIKE PRESTO.

Art Direction: **Daniel Weise**
Publishers: **Daniel Weise/Kalene Rivers**
Country: **USA**

SHERBERT

SHERBERT is something of a showcase for emerging illustrators, photographers, and writers. It began as an idea between two friends, Daniel Weise and Jenna Wilson, in Denver, Colorado, in the Summer of 2001. It is now based in Brooklyn, New York, and published by Daniel Weise and Kalene Rivers. Begun as a forum for Denver-based artists, it now features emerging talent from across the globe.

Targeted at 15 to 35 year olds interested in emerging talent and independent publishing, each issue of SHERBERT is loosely based on a theme—childhood, pastimes, and travel, for example—and is an open submission-based magazine. It does not contain traditional advertisements, but raises the money to fund each issue through sponsorships from small businesses, art entities, and individual donors.

The basic idea behind the design of the magazine is to make it very personal, by hand numbering and hand treating each cover, and letting the contributors' work be the focus. For each issue, two display faces are selected or designed by hand: for the Childhood issue, for instance, they used a custom stencil face designed by Luke Prowse from Research Studios in London. "We try and pair the typefaces loosely with the theme of the issue, so chose a stencil face to complement the theme of childhood," explains Weise. " Each issue is interesting in its own regard, from stenciling 800 covers in a single evening by myself to running all over town at the last minute on my bike, because my car wouldn't start, to find polybags," he adds. "Having a limited budget always leads to interesting things."

Jordin
9
Melinda
10

1984
Basit Khan

Art Direction: **Mark Gainor for Made**
Publisher: **Made Media**
Country: **Canada**

Made Magazine

Made was created by Raif Adelberg and Cathee Scrivano in 2001, as a 24-book series. The first issue was Number 24, and it has been published biannually, in reverse order, since then. Adelberg and Scrivano developed Made as a reaction to the lack of appropriate advertising venues for their retail shop at the time, and to support like-minded brands that also needed to push forward and evolve within the fashion industry.

"Made is like a living-room conversation," explains Michelle Evers from Made Media. "We showcase art, design, and ideas that we, the staff, like and are interested in. It's about luxury and distinguishable quality. We view the book as a design object unto itself. It needs to stand on its own as a design piece and then work as a more traditional book when you open its pages."

The art directors work with many high-profile creatives from around the world. The issue shown here includes a belly band designed by Kaws, featuring the distinctive X-eyed character that has become a cult classic. Kaws also created a pictorial for the magazine.

(See pages 150/151 for Issue 20 of Made.)

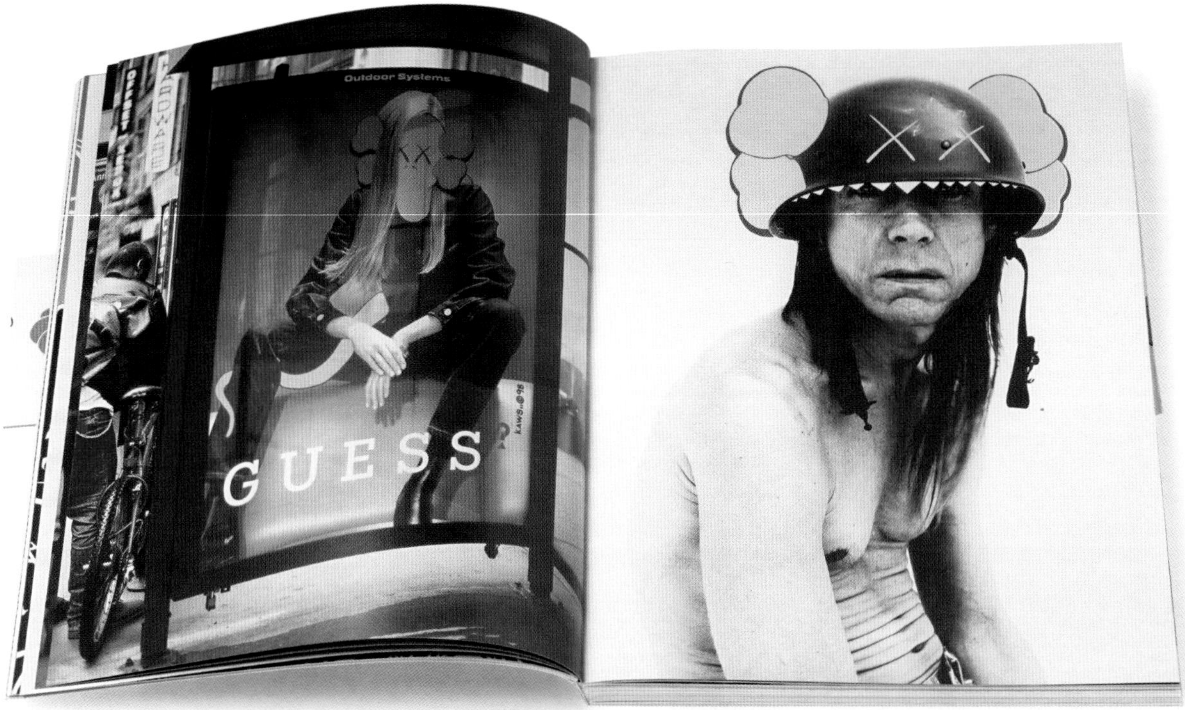

Phone
WRITERS

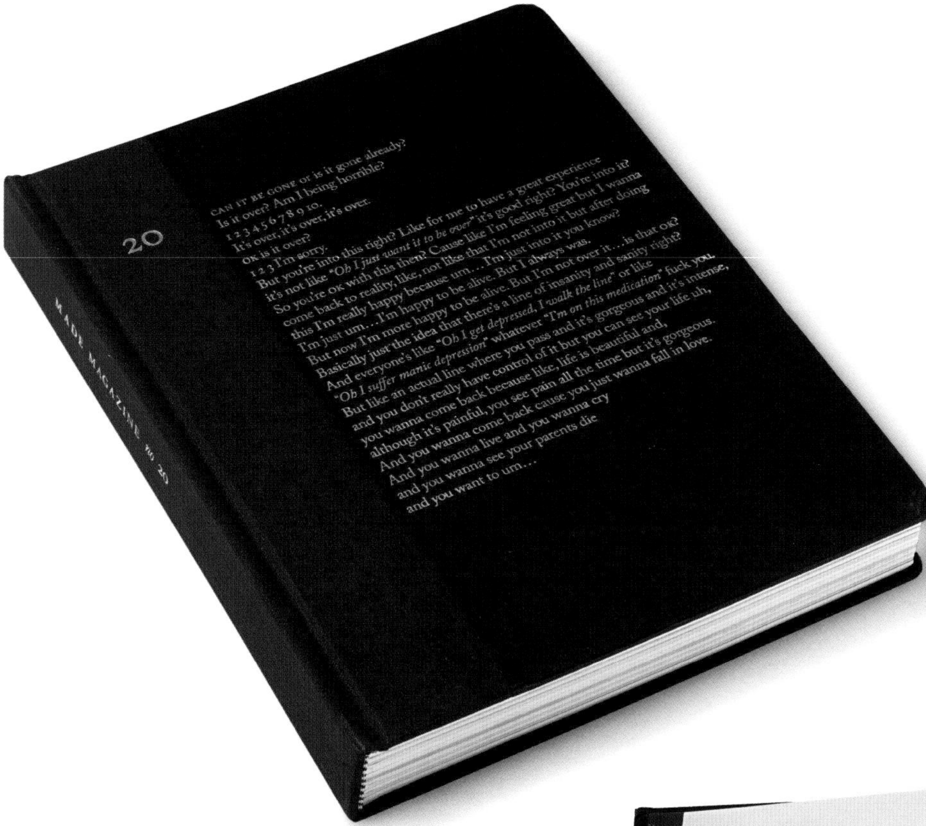

Art Direction: **Mark Gainor for Made**
Publisher: **Made Media**
Country: **Canada**

Made Magazine

This issue of Canadian magazine Made was inspired by vintage books. High-end production values, choice of paper stock—it features both coated and uncoated stocks—and inks give it a real sense of quality. It is bound with a hardback cover, canvas spine, and silver, foil-blocked Adobe Caslon Pro typeface. The theme continues inside with the contents and list of contributors laid out as they would be in a book.

The Made art directors have worked with many different artists for the issues published so far, including Kostas Seremetis, Ryan McGuinness, Kaws, Ricky Powell, Crash, and Bounty Hunter. Shown here are the spreads that Futura 2000 created for the magazine.

(See also page 148.)

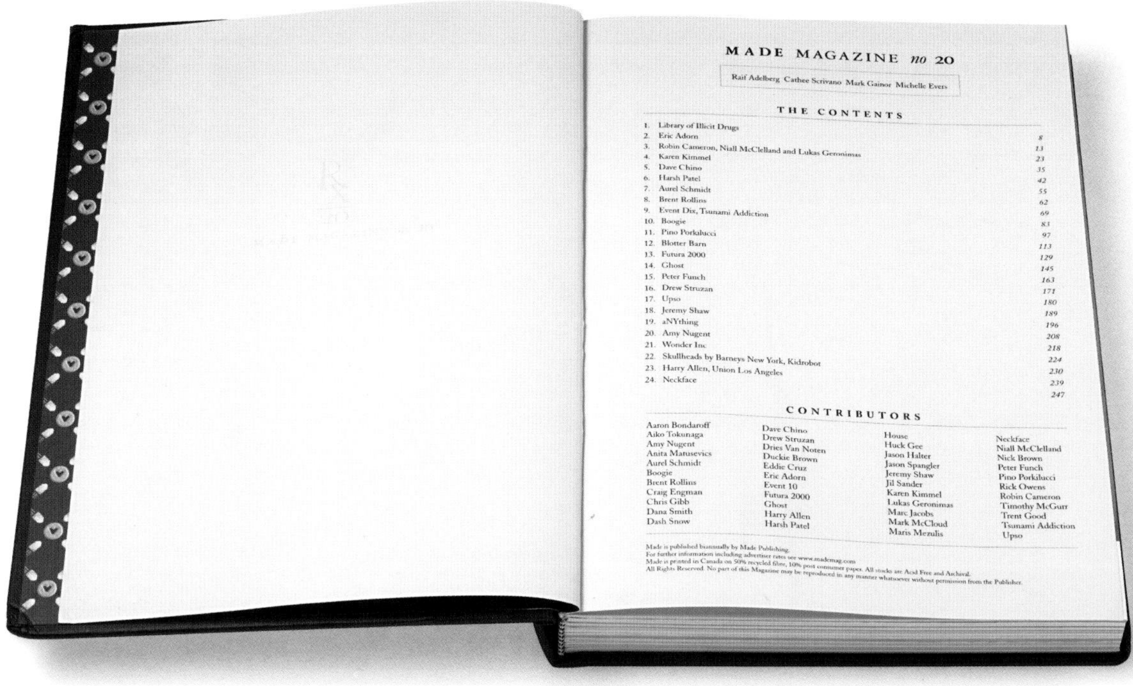

collecting
trading
tracking
saving
making
exchanging
object
park
interior
catalogue
exhibit
archive
concept
toy
exterior

Jonathan Barnbrook, Art Director and Designer, Kohkoku

What is the key to art directing a magazine?
Putting over the editorial content in an eye-catching way and making people understand what the articles are about. On a personal level, I am interested in pushing typography in magazine design. It's still an area that has a lot of potential.

Which magazine would you most like to art direct?
I don't think it would be a specific one, but I would like to have had the chance to have worked at the start of the Russian Revolution along with El Lissitzky, designing political magazines. It must have been a great time for experimentation.

What inspires your creativity?
My inspiration comes from lots of different sources. Bradbury Thompson said that to be a good typographer you must be interested in all aspects of life. I agree with this completely. Typography is about cultural exchange between people, the transference of meaning between two beings, and to do this you must be interested in culture, in life.

How important do you think the cover image on a magazine is?
It makes people pick up a magazine. A good cover sums up the magazine and catches the eye; a bad one confuses the reader as to what the magazine is about.

What is the future of magazine publishing?
The whole area is fragmenting. Within the next 20 years we will have a workable version of e-paper; the public now contribute to reporting news more than ever before; advertising models have broken down. It's going to be a difficult and exciting time for magazines.

Which is your favorite magazine, one that you collect?
I don't collect any magazines or anything else "designed." Things that influence me or interest me tend to be outside of commercial ephemera, such as literature or documentaries.

Giorgio De Mitri, Publisher, Editor, and Art Director, CUBE

What is the story behind CUBE?
CUBE began as a fanzine. It was distributed to kids in Italy and abroad for free. Sponsors paid for the printing and distribution. It quickly turned into a cult object and, in time, became a proper magazine. It then evolved into a bookzine—a biannual project—without sponsors, without articles or news. It became an album of the artists I respect, know, and work with; a catalog of contemporary moments, political movements, and personal reflections on life.

What inspires the creative idea behind each issue?
CUBE is a visual diary, an exaggerated and abstracted Moleskine. Each issue is a pure reflection of my state of mind at that time. CUBE is testimony to my personal relationships. It is about friendship, community, and an extended family.

How would you describe it in five words?
The first word: passions. CUBE is a vehicle for individual artists and photographers to show their passions in a non-commercial space. The second- and third-most important words: light and shadow. That is the way I look at photography. The fourth and fifth words: paper and ink. Experimenting with different papers and printing techniques is a process in itself.

How do you approach each issue?
It all begins by collecting images over time from friends and friends of friends. The images come by chance. Serendipity is the only word that describes this way of working. Making CUBE is like putting together a puzzle, only you don't know what the final image is supposed to be like. You have a sense of it, you've dreamed about it, but you really don't know what it is going to be until all the connections have been made. First, I gather together names and art projects, then I wait for the artworks to arrive. With all the pieces in hand, I begin arranging them in order, each one in relation to the other.

What is important about the team that you work with?
Their eyes, their hearts, and their minds.

How important do you think the cover image on a magazine is?
CUBE is not for sale. The cover doesn't have to attract buyers. We make our covers to please ourselves, not draw attention to ourselves or to hook an audience.

CUBE has some great covers. Can you tell me about them?
The first issue featured a photocollage by Thierry Ledé, the second a photocollage by Francesco Forti, the third is a photo by Enzo Ragazzini, and the last one is a collaboration between Phil Frost and Luca Bortolotti.

Which is your favorite magazine, one that you collect?
Too many to mention; I'm an avid magazine collector.

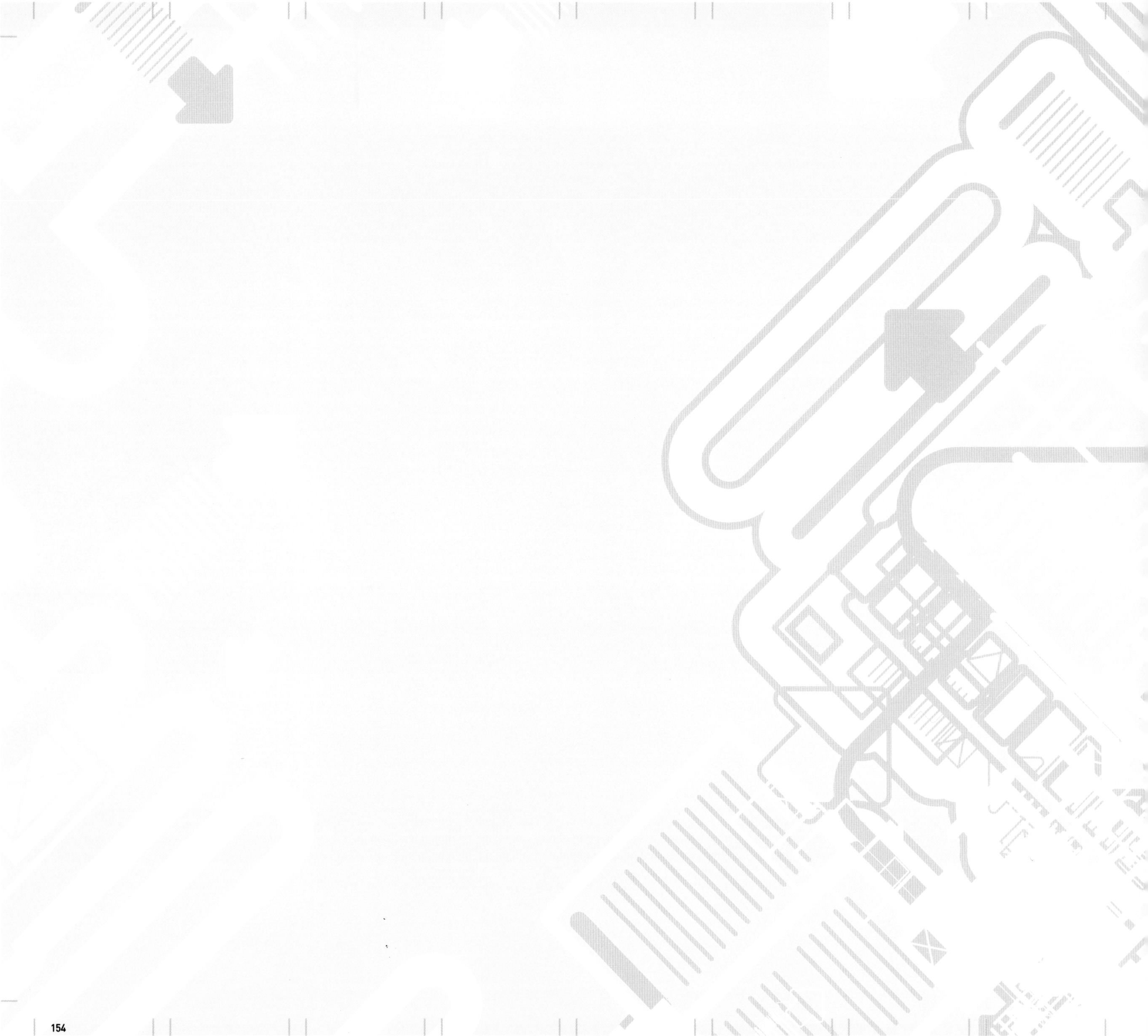

Contact Details & Acknowledgments

Contact Details

125
www.125magazine.com / info@125magazine.com

3 Deep Design
www.3deep.com.au / design@3deep.com.au

Amelia's magazine
www.ameliasmagazine.com / info@ameliasmagazine.com

Marc Atlan
www.marcatlan.com / info@marcatlan.com

AURA
aura@laki139.com

Sam Baker
sam@jmo-design.com

Barnbrook Design
www.barnbrook.net / us@barnbrook.net

BB/Saunders
www.bbsaunders.com / martin@bbsaunders.com

The Believer
www.believermag.com / letters@believermag.com

Blag
www.blagmagazine.com / blag@blagmagazine.com

Bulb
www.bulbmag.com / ana@bulbmag.com

Stella Bugbee
info@stellabugbee.com

Sebastian Campos
sebastian.campos@gmail.com

Carlos
www.jbcp.co.uk / jeremy.leslie@jbcp.co.uk

Centrefold
martin@bbsaunders.com

Andrew Clare
www.giantfieryhand.com / andrew@planbmag.com

Mark Constantine
mark@exitmagazine.co.uk

CUBE
www.cubemag.com / info@sartoria.com

Discover Upnorth
www.discover-upnorth.com / studio@discover-upnorth.com

Patrick Duffy
www.nodaysoff.com / patrick@nodaysoff.com

Sally A. Edwards
sae@blagmagazine.com

EI8HT
www.foto8.com / info@foto8.com

The End
www.endclub.com

Exit
www.exitmagazine.co.uk / info@exitmagazine.co.uk

Fairy Tale
www.fairytale-magazine.com / editor@fairytale-magazine.com

Flo
www.flomultizine.com / info@flomultizine.com

Frost Design
www.frostdesign.com.au / info@frostdesign.com.au

Full Moon Empty Sports Bag
www.fullmoonemptysportsbag.com
info@fullmoonemptysportsbag.com

Mark Gainor
www.mademag.com / mark@mademag.com

GeneveTokyo
www.genevetokyo.com / info@genevetokyo.com

Giampietro+Smith
info@studio-gs.com

GQ Style
www.gqstyle.com

Grafik.
www.grafikmagazine.co.uk / hello.grafik@gmail.com

GUM
www.gumworld.com / editors@gumworld.com

Half Empty
www.halfempty.com / info@halfempty.com

here and there
www.nakakobooks.com / nakakobooks@infoseek.jp

Ralf Herms
www.rosebud-inc.com / rh@rosebud-inc.com

HONEST
www.stayhonest.com / contact@stayhonest.com

Jalouse
e.pillault@editionsjalou.com

Justin Kay
www.industrial-organic.net / justin@industrial-organic.net

The Kitchen
www.thekitchen.co.uk / access@thekitchen.co.uk

LEMON
www.lemonland.net / info@lemonland.net

McSweeney's
www.mcsweeneys.net / letters@mcsweeneys.net

Martin Lötscher
www.soDA.ch / martin@soDA.ch

Lula
www.lulamag.com / me@lulamag.com

Made
www.mademag.com / michelle@mademag.com

MadeThought
www.madethought.com / info@madethought.com

Marmalade
www.marmaladeworld.com / mail@marmaladeworld.com

Me Magazine
www.memagazinenyc.com / office@memagazinenyc.com

Non-Format
www.non-format.com / info@non-format.com

Omagiu
www.omagiu.com / contact@omagiu.com

oneonenine
www.oneonenine.org / info@oneonenine.org

Plan B
www.planbmag.com / info@planbmag.com

Uscha Pohl
www.upandco.com / very@upandco.com

Poster
www.postermagazine.com.au / info@postermagazine.com.au

Refill
www.refillmag.com / refill@refillmag.com

+rosebud
www.rosebudmagazine.com / ask@rosebudmagazine.com

Sartoria
www.sartoria.com / info@sartoria.com

Saturday
www.saturday-london.com / info@saturday-london.com

self service
www.selfservicemagazine.com
editorial@selfservicemagazine.com

SHERBERT
www.sherbertmagazine.com / info@sherbertmagazine.com

Rebecca Smith
www.balconyjump.co.uk

Sneaker Freaker
www.sneakerfreaker.com / info@sneakerfreaker.com

soDA
www.soDA.ch / info@soDA.ch

spector cut+paste
www.spectormag.net / spector@spectormag.net

Marty Spellerberg
www.martyspellerberg.com / marty@halfempty.com

Inca Starzinsky
inca@muftimail.co.uk

Tank
www.tankmagazine.com / mail@tankmagazine.com

They Shoot Homos Don't They?
www.theyshoothomosdontthey.com
info@theyshoothomosdontthey.com

Tom Hingston Studio
www.hingston.net / info@hingston.net

Topic
www.topicmag.com / info@topicmag.com

Spencer Trace
sacha@marmaladeworld.com

Dario Utreras
www.diarizado.net / darioutreras@gmail.com

VERY
www.upandco.com / very@upandco.com

VICE
www.viceland.com / info@viceuk.com

Vier5
www.vier5.de / contact@vier5.de

Ani Watanabe
www.ninjafilms.tv / gtdesign@genevetokyo.com

Wire
www.thewire.co.uk / subs@thewire.co.uk

Woody
www.bigblockcreative.com / woody@bigblockcreative.com

Work in Progress
www.workinprogress.com / info@workinprogress.com

Zembla
www.zemblamagazine.com / vince@frostdesign.com.au

zingmagazine
www.zingmagazine.com / info@zingmagazine.com

Acknowledgments

In no particular order, I'd like to thank Ezra Petronio, Jonathan Barnbrook, Colin Metcalf, Marc Atlan, Amelia Gregory, and Tom Hingston for their time and contributions to this book. Of course, I would also like to thank all the other editors, publishers, art directors, and designers who allowed me to showcase their magazines in this book.

Thanks also to Xavier Young for the photography throughout, Simon Slater who has done an excellent design job, and Lindy Dunlop and the team at RotoVision for their support and assistance.

Special thanks to Jason.

This book is for Mum.

Index